THE ARTFUL TABLE

DONNA GORMAN AND

THE ARTF

PHOTOGRAPHS BY ELIZABETH HEYERT

ELIZABETH HEYERT

UL TABLE

WILLIAM MORROW AND COMPANY, INC., NEW YORK

It is the policy of William Morrow and Company, and its imprints and
affiliates, recognizing the importance of preserving what has been written, to print
the books we publish on acid-free paper, and we exert our best efforts to that end.

Library of Congress Cataloging-in-Publication Data
Gorman, Donna. The artful table / Donna Gorman and Elizabeth Heyert.
p. cm. ISBN 0-688-15204-X 1. Table setting and decoration.
I. Heyert, Elizabeth. II. Title. TX871.G67 1998 642' .8—dc21 98-3044 CIP

Printed in Singapore

First Edition

1 2 3 4 5 6 7 8 9 1 0

Book Design by Louise Fili and Mary Jane Callister, Louise Fili Ltd

www.williammorrow.com

FOR NANCY

donna gorman

FOR MY MOTHER, FLORENCE HEYERT

elizabeth heyert

Thank you

To Elizabeth Heyert, for her talented photography

To my editor, Justin Schwartz, for all of his thoughtful input, effort, and encouragement

To my agent, Barbara Hogenson, for her generous patience, perseverance, commitment,
and guidance throughout this amazing process of writing my first book

To Louise Fili, for contributing her ideas and talent

To Kathleen Hackett, who originally recognized and believed in our talent

To Gail Kinn, whose temporary involvement was always supportive and enthusiastic

To Sarah Feider, for her effort and enthusiasm, which I value as part of the whole

To Nicole Wise, whose help, ideas, and hard work I very much appreciate

To Ashleigh Blake for her talent, flexibility, and for keeping the candle burning on the other side

To Gina Federico, whose talent and commitment I have relied on for many years

To all of my very patient clients who put up with the many postponed deadlines and changing project schedules

To my good friends Nancy Brodlieb and Ingrid Leess, whose table settings are always inspired,
for generously lending objects from their own collections

Lastly, to my daughter Lilly, who helps me to see beauty in so many things

DONNA GORMAN

Many, many thanks to the creative team behind *The Artful Table*. Special thanks to our
wonderful designers, Louise Fili and Mary Jane Callister, who found elegant design solutions
to difficult problems and transformed my photographs into a beautiful book. My thanks to our editor
Justin Schwartz, who inherited this project in midstream and skillfully guided it through choppy
waters to publication. Also, my thanks to his helpful assistant, Cara Anselmo, to our art director,
Richard Oriolo, and to Janet Pedersen for her graceful illustrations. I am grateful to my longtime agent
and friend Barbara Hogenson for her hard work, encouragement, and dedication to bringing this book
to life, and for the thoughtful and enthusiastic participation of her assistant Sarah Feider. My warm thanks
to Margery Swigert for her empathy throughout this project and for her continuing friendship. And to
Doug Elliott, a.k.a. Harry, who always listens and understands, whose astute advice I value beyond measure,
and whose belief in the importance of a creative life is unwavering, my gratitude and love.

ELIZABETH HEYERT

COLOR SURROUNDS US. WE PERCEIVE COLORS CONSTANTLY, ALTHOUGH RARELY DO WE CON-SCIOUSLY DEFINE THEM AS COLORS. THE GLEAMING YELLOW OF EARLY MORNING SUNSHINE, DAPPLING OUR KITCHEN WALL, OR A SLASH OF CRIMSON ACROSS A TABLE AS THE SUN PASSES THROUGH A GLASS OF RED WINE—EACH IS AN ELEMENT OF THE COLOR PALETTE OF EVERYDAY LIFE. WHILE WE ARE HARDLY AWARE OF IT, COLOR PLUCKS AT OUR SENSES DAILY, SOOTHING

us, warming us, dazzling us, and luring us to it. Colors arouse feelings and recollections as resoundingly as certain tastes and sounds do. Colors often awaken the emotional landscape of our personal memory.

Imagine, then, the sensuous delight of working with color on a table designed for eating. As with any still life, color infiltrates and transforms each of the tables Donna and I create. We both have learned to respect its mysterious, evocative power. We continually experiment with colors, playing with their complex subtle relationships in much the same way that children do, before they become aware of artistic conventions or restrictions. We find that when we ignore the voices that tell us that particular colors clash, or are too bold, or too

somber, we often push our experiments into the realm of the unexpected. Playing with colors really means challenging our assumptions about what we like or dislike. Just as each of us, when we cook and eat, prefers certain flavors that characterize our unique tastes, an individual color palette emerges from within, from our private experience. Uncovering our personal aesthetic requires an open mind and the willingness to look, and look again, to recognize what feels inherently right.

The difficulty with seeing color is that we receive so much of it. Our senses are overwhelmed and overexposed. As we walk down a crowded city street, or look out of our living room window, the sheer quantity of color bombarding us can dull its impact. As artists, we learn visually to peel away layers of distracting color, instinctively to emphasize colors that subtly enhance familiar objects or scenes and transform our impressions of them. Still-life painters or photographers might spend hours rearranging the elements on their set, until an ideal symmetry among colors is achieved. A few blue plums on a pale green tablecloth, painted by Paul Klee, strikes us as hauntingly sad because of the shadowy relationship between the muted blues and greens. On the other hand, when Matisse paints plums, the interplay of his brilliant colors—his sensuous violet fruit, surrounded by a vibrant, crimson cloth, and bright yellow flowers—becomes a joyous celebration of simple, natural objects. By distilling the elements in these still-life paintings to a few extraordinary colors, both artists carry us into scenes of great but wildly different intensity.

Recently, on a visit to the Caribbean, I played a game with myself to sharpen my perceptions of the voluptuous colors around me. Like most photographers, I tend to see the world through a process of visual editing, drawing an imaginary frame around the subject in front of me. Anything outside the frame becomes irrelevant, but what remains inside the frame is isolated and enhanced. (The same effect can easily be created by forming a rectangle with your thumbs and forefingers, and looking through the empty space.) This way of seeing, similar to working within the borders of a canvas or looking through the lens of a camera, allows me to scrutinize the elements in any given setting by exaggerating their visual importance in my mind's eye.

Here are my notes, taken while sitting on a porch overlooking the flowering tropical landscape:

I see a pattern of fuchsia, yellow, and white flowers against a background of dark-green trees. When I move my frame to the left, the white and yellow flowers disappear from my view, leaving me with a palette of only pink and green. A move to the right, and the fuchsia flowers vanish. Now my frame includes only green leaves and pale delicate lavender blossoms, against a rough, gray stone path, with dark-green moss appearing in the cracks. Beautiful. A forty-five-degree turn, and the tropical palette returns in force. I see: red leaves variegated from russet color in the shadows to ruby where the sun passes through them; orange blossoms on a striped green stem; a flowering purple plant; lime-green bananas; yellow lemons against emerald-green leaves. When I turn to the left, the vibrant colors are gone. I see only violet shadows playing across the backs of gleaming white chairs on a faded taupe wood floor. A final shift, slightly to the right. The crystal-blue pool, dappled with ivory highlights from the sun. An icy palette of turquoise, spearmint, and white. A warm yellow-orange leaf floats across the surface of the water into the frame. The scene is transforming from cold emotion into a brighter, messier, and somehow more inviting picture.

My first impression of the landscape in St. Lucia—that it was a wild mélange of unruly color—missed most of the beautiful interplay among the dramatic hues. However, as I scrutinized colors isolated within my imagined frame, I began to intuitively feel which colors most strongly appealed to my unique sensibility. I envisioned color combinations, hot pinks with flaming oranges, and a palette restricted only to dozens of tropical greens. Certain of those colors sparked a visceral response, especially the primal greens, stirring my senses and my emotions, quite apart from the scene before me. This playful process of selecting a limited palette, then adding or subtracting colors as we sense how they react together, mirrors the way Donna and I manipulate color each time we create a table or a still life.

Seen through the eyes of someone else, the kaleidoscope of Caribbean colors might evoke sensations, memories, desires, and emotions completely different from my own. There are no right or wrong responses. I am drawn to and moved by a muted palette. Inspired by the landscape in St. Lucia, I might create a table on somber gray stone like the cracked garden path, using accents mimicking the mournful, understated hues of the lavender flowers and rich green moss. Donna prefers a more vibrant palette, such as fuchsia and lime green, so for a table she might extract only two colors from the riotous color scheme. Someone else might revel in the sensuous excess of the entire tropical color spectrum, even though I perceived it as gaudy. Each encounter with color resonates in our memory, adding layers to the palette we drift toward and feel comfortable with. A personal aesthetic grows from the sensory memory as we look around us and are visually engaged.

Begin to gaze at food through an artist's eyes—at the brilliant red of a lobster, the fleshy pink inside a ripe fig, and the luminous green of fresh grapes. Notice unusual natural colors, such as the orange-and-red-dappled skin of blood oranges, or the ruby color of a sliced pomegranate. Scatter the flame-colored oranges onto a faded turquoise platter, and see if they seem different to you, floating on the cool blue background. Now, imagine colors you associate with a specific time, such as the traditional red and green of Christmas. If the red was the color of bricks, and the green was the color of a Granny Smith apple, would you still think of Christmas? For me, that chalky terra-cotta color paired with the acid apple green evokes a sun-drenched desert, or a Mediterranean afternoon. Color affects everyone differently, but each color we incorporate in a table will subtly alter the emotional experience of being there.

For an artist, color remains unequaled as a visual tool for extracting the emotional essence from any setting. Consider Manet's floral still lifes, those magical bouquets that he painted in the final year of his life. In these last paintings, Manet abandons himself to color and light, transforming a rather hackneyed subject into a metaphor for beauty, purity, and the brevity of life. A pink rose is not simply solid pink but a mysterious amalgam of subtle hues from harsh reds to salmon and ivory. The artist blends the colors delicately, so that the flowers sparkle with freshness. Yet upon closer scrutiny, the unusual palette feels slightly jarring, creating an impression of sharpness with undertones that are dry rather than sweet. In a yellow rose, burnt orange, mustard, and murky brown hues gleam, soft and lush,

against the strange, primeval green of their leaves. These luxuriant flowers, painted in odd, unnatural colors, also appear astringent, perhaps with a tart perfume. The tension created by Manet's skillful manipulation of color resonates in an emotionally charged still life. We see a poignantly bittersweet view of beauty in nature, through the eyes of a dying man.

Allow yourself time to observe the interplay of colors in your immediate surroundings, and begin to discover what colors kindle your emotions. Looking around me, I see a patchwork of indigo and magenta shadows mingling with the brilliant orange of the late-afternoon sun on my studio wall. These glowing colors form a vital palette that fleetingly describes and energizes this portion of my day. As the sun sets, I watch the orange fade into salmon, and the magenta and indigo blend into a soft pool of purple. For reasons I do not fully understand, these colors stir an emotional response within me, perhaps because of the transitory nature of their beauty. When we look at the panorama of color around us, we may experience a golden jolt of perception, of the elegant nature of everyday objects when they are imbued with light or shadow. This is the essence of still life, to elevate familiar elements into forms that intensify our understanding and awareness of them, and to enable us to experience them with an unbiased vision.

CREATING A MONOCHROMATIC TABLE
USING ALL WARM HUES

suggested menu: STRIPS OF ROASTED YELLOW PEPPERS SERVED OVER DANDELION GREENS

GOLDEN BUTTERNUT SQUASH RISOTTO FLECKED WITH LARGE SHAVINGS OF PARMESAN CHEESE AND FRESH SAGE

CRUSTY LOAVES OF YELLOW SEMOLINA BREAD SERVED WITH PLENTY OF GOLDEN OLIVE OIL

ELEMENTS

HAND-PAINTED YELLOW
WATERCOLOR PAPER

YELLOW COTTON
BATISTE FABRIC

OVERSIZED CHUNK
OF PARMESAN CHEESE

HAND-GLAZED
CERAMIC PLATES

ANTIQUE LABORATORY
BEAKER FILLED WITH
GOLDEN OLIVE OIL

WOODEN CUTLERY

HANDBLOWN WINEGLASSES

CREAM-COLORED
PILLAR CANDLES

BRANCH OF LEMONS

YELLOW CERAMIC DISH
OF GREEN OLIVES

COARSELY WOVEN
YELLOW NAPKINS

WHEN
THE **FABRIC**
OVERLAPS THE
PAPER, COLOR IS
INTENSIFIED.

LEAVE **EDGES OF**
PAPER EXPOSED.

PILLAR CANDLES
SIT DIRECTLY
ON THE TABLE.

NO FLOWERS

BRANCH OF
MEYER LEMONS

BUNCH AND
LAYER **FABRIC**
OVER PAPER...
DRAPED VS.
FLAT...

OVERSIZED
YELLOW CERAMIC
PLATES

LARGE PARMESAN CHEESE SITS DIRECTLY ON THE PAPER . . . CENTERS THE TABLE.

USE PAPER ON TABLE SURFACE AS RECEPTACLE FOR BREADS AND CHEESES.

EXPOSING WOODEN TABLE SURFACE ADDS WARMTH TO THE SETTING.

NATURAL ELEMENTS CHEESE, BREAD, LEMONS, OIL, OLIVES.

USE FOOD AND VARIOUS OBJECTS ON THE TABLE TO "LAYER" SHADES OF YELLOW.

USE COLOR TO EVOKE THE FEELING OF WARMTH.

MIX SHADES OF YELLOW.

SHADES OF WARM-YELLOW HUES OF VARYING INTENSITY.

TALL WINE-GLASSES ADD SOME FORMALITY TO A RUSTIC SETTING.

painting notes: APPLY WATERED-DOWN YELLOW WATERCOLOR PAINT TO PAPER SURFACE USING A SOFT-BRISTLED BRUSH. APPLY COATS WITH VARYING SHADES OF YELLOW . . . LET THE PATINA EVOLVE . . . KEEP THE PAINT TRANSLUCENT, NOT TOO HEAVY.

LIMITING THE PALETTE TO THREE COLORS:

GREEN, RED, AND YELLOW

suggested menu: YELLOW LEMON CURD TART SPRINKLED WITH FRESH RASPBERRIES

or

HONEY ICE CREAM SERVED WITH ROASTED NECTARINES

HOMEMADE BITTERSWEET CHOCOLATE TRUFFLES DUSTED WITH COCOA POWDER

A GOOD SAUTERNE WINE

LIMITING THE PALETTE TO THREE

ELEMENTS

PAINTED CANVAS

LARGE TI LEAVES

OVERSIZED GLASS PLATES

LINEN NAPKINS

GREEN PORCELAIN BOWL

GREEN ART NOUVEAU
CERAMIC VASE

SMALL FUNNEL-SHAPED
GLASSES

ITALIAN GRAPPA BOTTLE

ANTIQUE SILVER DESSERT
FORKS AND KNIVES WITH
MOTHER-OF-PEARL HANDLES

ROSES

OVERSIZED GLASS PLATES "WEIGHT DOWN" LEAVES.

FRUIT AND PASTRY APPEAR TO BE SITTING DIRECTLY ON THE LEAVES.

DESSERT SERVED ON OVERSIZED PLATES SEEMS MORE SPECIAL.

ANTIQUE CUTLERY, VASES, AND FINE LINEN NAPKINS CONTRAST WITH THE INFORMAL CANVAS AND GLASS.

LET **CONFETTI ROSES** OPEN . . . PETALS SCATTERED AROUND TABLE SURFACE — ROMANTIC.

MIX DIFFERENT SHADES OF GREEN WITH THE OBJECTS ON THE TABLE . . . VASES . . . BOWLS . . . NAPKINS . . . TABLE COVERING . . .

CONTRASTING **REFINED ELEMENTS** WITH ROUGH, **EARTHY ELEMENTS** MAKES THE TABLE DESIGN MORE INTERESTING.

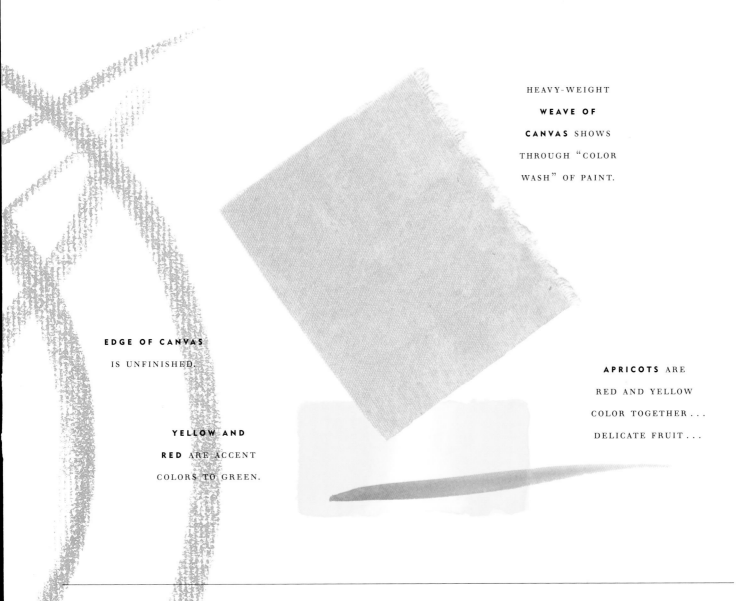

HEAVY-WEIGHT **WEAVE OF CANVAS** SHOWS THROUGH "COLOR WASH" OF PAINT.

EDGE OF CANVAS IS UNFINISHED.

APRICOTS ARE RED AND YELLOW COLOR TOGETHER... DELICATE FRUIT...

YELLOW AND RED ARE ACCENT COLORS TO GREEN.

painting notes: WATER DOWN DESIRED COLOR OF ACRYLIC PAINT TO THE CONSISTENCY OF MILK. APPLY WITH A LARGE MEDIUM-BRISTLED BRUSH. APPLY MULTIPLE COATS UNTIL DESIRED SHADE IS ACHIEVED. THE MORE COATS APPLIED, THE DARKER THE SHADE OF COLOR... KEEP PAINT THINNED WITH WATER, ALLOWING THE FABRIC GRAIN TO SHOW THROUGH.

USING PRIMARY COLORS IN A
FLUID RATHER THAN GEOMETRIC SETTING

suggested menu: YELLOW TOMATO GAZPACHO SOUP GARNISHED WITH RED PEPPERS

A DELICATE SALAD OF MÂCHE GREENS TOSSED WITH A TART LEMON VINAIGRETTE

FRESH ASPARAGUS FRITTATA, SERVED WITH STEAMED NEW POTATOES AND GENEROUS WEDGES
OF TOASTED COUNTRY BREAD SPREAD WITH FRESH CHÈVRE AND DRIZZLED WITH HONEY

or

FRESH PASTA TOSSED WITH PESTO SAUCE MADE FROM ARUGULA AND FRESH BASIL LEAVES

ELEMENTS

WOOD TABLE SURFACE

RED LINEN FABRIC

VARYING HAND-
GLAZED YELLOW CERAMIC
DINNER PLATES

BLUE HANDMADE
CERAMIC BOWL

COBALT-BLUE GLASS
CARAFE AND GLASSES

TALL HANDMADE
CERAMIC VASE

RED GLASS VOTIVES

GLASS CAKE STAND

PRESSED-GLASS SUGAR BOWL

STAINLESS STEEL
CUTLERY WITH BLACK
PATINATED HANDLES

RED LINEN NAPKINS

BUNCH AND
ARRANGE **RED
LINEN** DOWN
CENTER OF THE
TABLE...NOT
MESSY...FABRIC
CREATES A FLOW,
MOTION...NOT
RIGID AND FLAT.

RANDOMLY
SCATTER **ORANGES
AND STAR FRUIT**
AROUND PRIMARY-
COLORED OBJECTS
...UNRIPENED
STAR FRUIT IS A
BEAUTIFUL SHADE
OF GREEN.

RED

**BRIGHTLY
COLORED
OBJECTS** CARRY
COLORS IN A
FLOW DOWN THE
TABLE...DON'T
ARRANGE ANY-
THING RIGIDLY.

LET **TABLE**
HAVE A FLOW...
MOVEMENT.

**GLASSES AND
CARAFE** FROM
FINLAND...
MODERN DESIGN...

YELLOW

BLUE

PALETTE
EMPHASIZES
PRIMARY COLORS
USED IN AN UNEX-
PECTED WAY.

TALL HANDMADE VASE ADDS AN EARTHY BUT
SOPHISTICATED QUALITY... OFF-CENTER PLACEMENT ADDS
TO THE "MOTION" AND INTEREST OF THE TABLE DESIGN.

RANDOMLY PLACE **YELLOW DINNER PLATES**... KEEP SEATING
CASUAL... NOT RIGID... A SENSE OF MOVEMENT.

WRAP **STRIPS OF STRAW RAFFIA** AROUND BASE OF
GLASS CAKE STAND... ELEVATED RECEPTACLE FOR THE ORANGES.

KEEP **TABLE**
DESIGN SENSUAL,
NOT JUVENILE OR
"MONDRIANLIKE."

HANDMADE JAPANESE CERAMIC BOWL... "SOPHISTICATED-EARTHY"

RED GLASS VOTIVES "FALL AWAY" ONTO RED LINEN.

SOPHISTICATED MIXTURE OF **MACHINE AND HANDMADE**
OBJECTS KEEPS TABLE INTERESTING.

NO NEED TO
SEW OR FINISH
THE EDGES OF
THE FABRIC.

EXPOSE **WOOD SURFACE** ON BOTH SIDES OF TABLE... NOT MESSY...
FABRIC CREATES A FLOW, MOTION... NOT RIGID AND FLAT.

[23]

ADDING COLOR TO A TABLE BY
LAYERING MULTICOLORED GLASS

suggested menu: SMALL PLATES OF APPETIZERLIKE TAPAS: TINY BALLS OF
SOFT CHEESE ROLLED IN MINCED FRESH HERBS, STEAMED ASPARAGUS, BITE-SIZE
POTATO CAKES TOPPED WITH MARINATED CODFISH, ROASTED SHALLOTS AND GARLIC
SERVED ON SLICES OF TOASTED CIABATTA BREAD BRUSHED WITH OLIVE OIL

or

A CLOUDLIKE CHEESE SOUFFLÉ SERVED WITH A SALAD OF DELICATE
MIXED GREENS, TOSSED IN CHAMPAGNE VINAIGRETTE, AND POACHED PEACHES

LARGE SHAVINGS OF WHITE CHOCOLATE SERVED WITH ALMOND TUILES

ELEMENTS

WHITE SHEER
ORGANZA FABRIC

HANDBLOWN
GLASS VESSELS

GREEN GLASS PLATES

YELLOW GLASSES

WHITE SILK
SHANTUNG NAPKINS

STERLING SILVER
FLATWARE

BALLOONLIKE **ART GLASS** BECOMES THE FOCUS OF THE TABLE DISPLAY.

WHEN THE **COLORS OF THE GLASS OVERLAP,** THEY CREATE MORE COMPLEX COLORS...LESS NAIVE...THIS EFFECT MAKES THE TABLE MORE SOPHISTICATED.

SIMPLE "MACHINE-MADE" PLATES AND GLASSES ARE IN MORE COMPLEX COLORS, NOT SO SWEET...A NICE CONTRAST TO THE STRONG CLEAN COLORS OF THE ART GLASS.

LAYERS OF STRONG COLOR FILL THE TABLE...VERY DRAMATIC.

KEEPING THE **PLACE SETTINGS** ON ONE SIDE OF THE TABLE MAKES THE ART GLASS THE FOCUS.

HANDMADE QUALITY OF GLASS VESSELS IS A A NICE CONTRAST TO PLATES AND GLASSES.

GLASS VESSELS CAN BE USED FOR SERVING WATER AND WINE.

COLORS OF GLASS VESSELS . . . MIX AS MANY COLORS AS POSSIBLE . . . VARY HEIGHT.

KEEP **TABLE DESIGN** SIMPLE . . . KEEP FOCUS ON THE ILLUSION FROM ALL OF THE COLOR . . .

USING FINE **SILK NAPKINS AND STERLING FLATWARE** ADDS FORMALITY TO THE SIMPLE DESIGN.

LET **FABRIC** "BUNCH UP" A LITTLE . . . ALMOST CLOUD-LIKE . . . SOFT.

LIGHT PASSING THROUGH THE GLASS ENHANCES ITS JEWEL-LIKE QUALITIES.

UNHEMMED, **WHITE SILK ORGANZA FABRIC** LAID CASUALLY OVER THE TABLE SURFACE . . .

USING PASTEL COLORS WITHOUT CREATING
A CHILDLIKE OR SWEET SETTING

suggested menu: POACHED SALMON SERVED WITH WHITE ASPARAGUS
AND CELADON GREEN–COLORED BASIL MAYONNAISE

GOAT CHEESE AND LEEK TART

ASSORTED PASTEL COLOR SORBETS LIKE APRICOT, LEMON, AND MINT

or

SHRIMP, POACHED WITH FRESH GINGER AND LEMONGRASS, THEN SERVED
OVER SLICED CUCUMBER AND CELLOPHANE RICE NOODLES

ELEMENTS

STONE TABLE SURFACE

TINTED PINK AND
LAVENDER MEXICAN
BARK PAPER

GREEN-GLAZED
STEINER PLATES

OVERSIZED BLUE TUSCAN
CERAMIC PLATTER

JAPANESE PORCELAIN
CUPS AND BOWLS IN
ASSORTED COLORS

LOW CRYSTAL WINEGLASSES

YELLOW ART NOUVEAU
GLASS VASE

GOLDEN-COLORED
SILK NAPKINS

SIMPLE SILVER CUTLERY

COMBINE AN ASSORTED **PALETTE OF SOFT, CHALKY PASTEL COLORS,** TYPICALLY USED IN IMPRESSIONIST SKETCHES.

RESTRICT **CERAMIC COLORS** TO SHADES OF BLUE, GREEN, AND YELLOW . . .

MULTIPLE GREEN-COLORED STONEWARE PLATES GIVE TABLE CONSISTENCY.

MIXING SIZE, COLOR, AND TYPE OF **CERAMIC ACCESSORIES** KEEPS TABLE INTERESTING . . . MIX CERAMICS THAT ARE BOTH EARTHY AND REFINED.

ROSÉ WINE IN LOW CRYSTAL GLASSES ADDS COLOR.

TRANSLUCENT YELLOW-COLORED ART NOUVEAU VASE IS ELEGANT . . . INTERESTING RECEPTACLE FOR WATER OR WINE.

EXPOSE **STONE TABLE SURFACE**... GIVES WEIGHT TO THE SOFT PASTEL COLORS...KEEPS THEM FROM APPEARING TOO SWEET.

THREE OR FOUR LARGE SHEETS OF **PINK AND LAVENDER HANDMADE PAPER** COVER THE TABLE SURFACE. ARRANGE LOOSELY... NOT RIGID...

KEEP **TABLE DESIGN** SOPHIS- TICATED, NOT JUVENILE.

YELLOW AND PINK PLUMS SCATTERED AROUND TABLE SURFACE SUR- ROUNDING THE BLUE AND GREEN CERAMICS ARE BETTER THAN FLOWERS.

GOLDEN- COLORED SILK NAPKINS... ELEGANT ACCENT...

HANDMADE PAPER HAS A MORE COMPLEX PATINA THAN SOLID-COLORED PAPER... IT'S MORE INTER- ESTING.

...**THE PAPER** ACTS LIKE TRADITIONAL PLACE MATS, ADDING DESIGN AND PROTECTING THE TABLE SUR- FACE...DEFINING THE SPACE...

[35]

TRANSFORMING A NEUTRAL SETTING
WITH ONE STRONG COLOR

suggested menu: ROASTED EGGPLANT SOUP

SALAD OF RADICCHIO AND ENDIVE LEAVES DRIZZLED WITH AGED BALSAMIC VINEGAR

SAUTÉED BREAST OF DUCK WITH A BLACK CURRANT SAUCE SERVED WITH ROSEMARY POTATO GALETTE

PLUM ICE CREAM MADE WITH ARMAGNAC AND SERVED WITH CHOCOLATE BISCOTTI

ELEMENTS

GALVANIZED-STEEL
TABLE SURFACE

PURPLE TAFFETA FABRIC

HANDMADE CHARCOAL-
COLORED CERAMIC PLATES

MUSSEL SHELLS

SILVER COFFEE URN
AND CANDY DISH

CRYSTAL FOOTED
CANDY DISH

PURPLE GLASSES

STAINLESS FLATWARE

ALLIUM FLOWERS

MIX VARIOUS
"FLEA-MARKET"
SILVER PIECES...
LEAVE TARNISHED
PATINA...AGED
ELEGANCE ADDS
INTEREST.

CASUALLY STACK
ALLIUM FLOWERS
ON CRYSTAL CANDY
DISH...ADDS
HEIGHT...
CARRIES PURPLE
COLOR OFF TABLE
SURFACE.

HANDMADE
DINNER PLATES...
GLOSSY CHARCOAL-
COLORED GLAZE...
INFORMAL BUT
ELEGANT...

USE A VERY
STRONG **ACCENT**
COLOR.

REFLECTIVE
METAL TABLE
SURFACE HIGH-
LIGHTS METAL
OBJECTS ON TABLE
...SHEEN FROM
TAFFETA...
IRIDESCENCE OF
MUSSEL SHELLS.

BUNCH **FABRIC** DOWN CENTER OF TABLE — WEIGHT DOWN PUFFY AREAS WITH SERVING PIECES... CREATES A FLOW OF COLOR.

CASUALLY PILE **SHELLS OVER CLOTH**... EXPOSE INSIDE OF SHELL...IRIDESCENT COLOR... PILE OF SHELLS INTERSECTS THE VERTICAL FLOW OF DRAPED CLOTH.

MUSSEL SHELLS COLLECTED FROM THE SEASHORE — SOAK, SCRUB, AND DRY IN THE SUN.

SHEEN AND DEPTH OF FABRIC COLOR... TWO DIFFERENT WOVEN THREADS, PURPLE AND BLACK

UNDERSIDE OF MUSSEL SHELLS IS A SURPRISE OF SOFT COLOR.

A FEW YARDS OF **COLORED TAFFETA FABRIC,** BUNCHED AND DRAPED OVER METAL SURFACE ...ALL OTHER ELEMENTS BECOME A TEXTURAL BACKDROP.

KEEP **UNFINISHED EDGE.**

A JAPANESE ARTIST PAINTS AN INDIGO CIRCLE ON A WHITE PORCELAIN PLATE. THAT SOLITARY SPLASH OF COLOR CREATES A PATTERN. PATTERNS FORM WHEN CLEAR BEADS OF RAIN SPATTER A WINDOW OR WHEN A SEAGULL LEAVES A DELICATE TRAIL OF PRINTS IN THE SAND. A PATTERN CAN BE ARTIFICIAL—MADE ON A SURFACE BY BRUSH STROKES OR A PRINTING PRESS—OR OCCUR NATURALLY, AS IN THE VEINS OF A LEAF. PATTERN CONSISTS OF ENDLESS REPETITION

or a few straight lines; geometric squares or organic curves as fluid as water on a shore. Like the ink blots of a Rorschach test, the nature of pattern is representational—it reminds us of other things.

Unlike color, which affects us viscerally in subtle and mysterious ways, pattern charges the air like static electricity. Pattern shouts its presence. When Donna and I experiment with pattern on a table, we inevitably find ourselves wrestling with a dynamic energy that seems to be intrinsic to pattern, as well as with certain universal visual associations. Instead of allowing any pattern to overpower our idea, we continually play with ways to defuse the cliché inherent in its style. Often our experiments involve confusing the eye—mixing odd elements such as traditional patterned china with a cold, metallic surface; or using a sweet pattern of flowers or prosaic checks in an unsentimental setting. Sometimes we isolate a particularly forceful pattern that has been printed or painted on a surface so that we emphasize its innate intensity; then we counterbalance it with a selection of gritty, textural elements that as a collection create an amorphous, random pattern. By playing with contradictory elements, looking at atypical combinations, and trying to keep an open mind about what we see, we can rattle conventional expectations about what any pattern should mean to us.

All patterns, from the most realistic copy of a recognizable object (such as a leaf pattern) to the most abstract (such as an ink blot), trigger connections that flood our senses with traditional or symbolic messages. Patterns push our buttons, not in the way that color does by awakening emotion, but because they remind us of the familiar. When I see a blue-and-white-check pattern on a tablecloth, I remember summer afternoons with corn on the cob, watermelon, and relay races. And a certain kind of red-and-white stripe always makes me think of peppermint candy, even if I see it on a dress or on a beach umbrella. These vivid sensory associations, some of which stretch back into our personal histories, and some of which reflect a more primal experience, make pattern a potent device for an artist to harness, then subvert in imaginative ways.

Still-life painters and photographers relish the sensory drama inherent in the complicated nature of pattern. Many of the meticulous Northern Baroque still life paintings include curious, even bizarre, patterned objects among the elements. I always feel a slight jolt of voyeuristic delight when I spot them. These devices—the iridescent ovals of an exotic peacock feather draped beside a few delicate pots and lacy crystal jars; the yawning mouth of a huge striped shell tucked among leather books and stone jugs; the patterned fleshy rings of crimson raw salmon; the marbled pattern of pink raw meat on a counter; or the rosy seeds of a succulent pomegranate, unexpectedly cut open in a prosaic bowl of fruit—all are patterns that surprise the eye and, especially, titillate the senses. The addition of pattern in each of these paintings transports the subject matter beyond decorative realism into a gorgeous world of sensuality and desire.

Like some painters, photographers play with patterns using light and shadow—graphic tricks of the eye that can elevate ordinary objects into complex, even disturbing abstractions. In a famous photograph from the 1920s, the photographer Paul Outerbridge transforms a plain Saltine cracker box, stripped of its wrapper, into an unreal pattern of shapes that appear to be floating in space. He creates strange triangular patterns from the play of strong light across the bland, rectangular surface of the box, so as to alter our perceptions of what we are looking at. These patterns, which seem to be reflections, or mirror images, or possibly blocks of empty space, challenge our sense of what really exists, and what is an illusion. Outerbridge invites us to draw our response to this eerie, abstract image from the deep well of our associative memory.

While Outerbridge created patterns of light in his studio, most of us have seen similar abstract patterns outside, on a beautiful day—when strong sunlight pours through the twists and curls of a wrought-iron balcony, for example. As you walk down the street, scrutinize the landscape the way a photographer does. Each time you discover an unconventional pattern in your surroundings, take a series of mental snapshots. Often I will remember a dramatic pattern made by the light of a lamp, or fallen leaves, or broken twigs long after I have seen it, and be inspired to experiment with similar elements when I next create a still life. Look for unusual or beautiful patterns of abstract light and dark—the dappled-shadow pattern of willow leaves on the geometric surface of a brick path, or the hard-edged blocks of golden afternoon light making a checkerboard pattern on a slate terrace. You will notice certain times of the day when patterns of light dazzle and enliven the most banal office wall, or an ordinary concrete sidewalk. Watching patterns of light is an easy and obvious

way to learn about the extraordinary transformative energy that all pattern generates—but pattern, from any source, can enhance and alter the way we see our immediate environment.

Begin to discover the natural patterns in your surroundings, especially patterns that resonate with sensory associations—outlandish abstract configurations inside and outside seashells, or the graphic ribbons of dried seaweed on pale sand, at the beach; or the veined and grainy surface of stones after a rain. Notice odd or unusual patterns on fruits and vegetables—the wavy yellow lines on the skin of a Korean melon; the jagged shell of an artichoke; the striations of fuchsia and white of radicchio; dotted cactus pears; the abstract splashes of emerald green and cream on the plump surface of dumpling squash. Cut some of these open, revealing sensuous patterns of seeds and stones. What do the strange, evocative patterns remind you of? Then, experiment, as we do, by creating random patterns with simple materials—such as a collection of those tactile stones, or some striped tropical leaves, or Forelle pears, whose skins are naturally spattered with a gorgeous pattern of rose and gold. Roll the pears onto one end of a plain table. The bare surface will metamorphose into a vibrant asymmetrical design of natural color. Or layer a few slender blades of sea grass across a stainless-steel surface, and watch what happens as their graceful shapes are reflected in the shiny surface. The mirrored image multiplies and repeats the pattern of grass like a ripple of patterned light on water. The beauty of random pattern is elusive and spontaneous. Like the mesmerizing patterns of a kaleidoscope, they form and re-form but are virtually impossible to replicate at another time or in another setting.

The great Surrealist painter and photographer Man Ray managed to duplicate the fleeting visual energy of a random pattern, translating it into a masterly painting. Early in his career, while he was cutting out shapes from construction paper for a collage of dancers, he spotted the discarded remnants of colored paper arranged by accident on his studio floor. They intrigued him precisely because he had not preconceived the careless pattern of their composition. To Man Ray, the configuration of those fragments of simple paper seemed to radiate with the freeform energy he associated with dancing. He selected six abstract scraps from the floor, arranged them in layers for maximum color contrast, then faithfully re-created the pattern in trompe-l'oeil on his canvas. This realistic rendering of scraps of wastepaper became a painting about the shadowy dynamic of bodies in motion. Man Ray felt the fugitive, rhythmic movements of dance were encapsulated in the random patterns born of chance discovery.

This is the creative challenge of pattern: how to channel the sensory experiences it evokes so that we can exploit the theater of our associations. Matisse did it in a deceptively simple still life that illustrates the artist's brilliant use of pattern to alter the perceptions of his audience. Matisse painted five unconnected objects, then added pattern to their surfaces where realistically no pattern should be—dots and dashes on a yellow seashell, wavy stripes across a purple pitcher, and a variegated crown of patterned leaves around a small white magnolia flower. By the application of pattern to these uncomplicated objects, Matisse seemingly sets them in motion. Like the many airborne balls of a master juggler, each patterned element seems to exist in its own energy field, and to connect, against all reason, with the other vibrating elements. The result is a painting of a commonplace subject—a still life of a flower on a table—elevated into a passionate moment of great theater.

When you incorporate pattern in a table, think about exciting the senses. All still life is, in many ways, about awakening memory and desire. Pattern, with its innate energy, and its power to evoke buried sensations and distant experience, provides a channel to the imagination. Play with pattern, with an unbiased vision, and you will be surprised, as we often are, about where it will lead you.

MIXING PATTERNS WITHIN A LIMITED
PALETTE OF BLACK AND WHITE

suggested menu: COLORFUL SPANISH PAELLA: YELLOW-COLORED SAFFRON RICE
PATTERNED WITH MUSSELS, CLAMS, SHRIMP, CHORIZO SAUSAGE, STRIPS OF ROASTED
RED PEPPERS, AND FRESH GREEN PEAS SERVED WITH TOASTED GARLIC BREAD

or

A SALAD OF BLOOD ORANGE AND FENNEL SLICES SERVED OVER A BED OF ARUGULA

RUSTIC PROVENÇAL DUCK STEW DOTTED WITH BLACK AND
GREEN OLIVES AND SERVED WITH BLACK LENTILS

ELEMENTS

BLACK-AND-CREAM-
COLORED FABRICS

STONE TABLE SURFACE

HAND-GLAZED WHITE
CERAMIC PLATES

POLISHED GRAY-COLORED
STONES

LOW CLEAR CRYSTAL
GLASSES

HAND-PAINTED ACOMA
POTTERY VASE

OVERSIZED STAINLESS
CUTLERY

NAPKINS

TABLECLOTH

LAYER **FABRIC PATTERNS.**

MIX AS MANY **MONOCHROMATIC PATTERNS** AS POSSIBLE.

FABRIC IN TWO SCALES . . . PRINTED DESIGNS LOOK WOVEN.

PATTERNS APPEAR TO BE ALMOST TEXTURAL.

SOLID-COLORED WHITE PLATES BREAK UP PATTERN . . .
GIVE RELIEF FROM THE DESIGN . . . NONRIGID PLACEMENT
IS MORE INTERESTING, LESS EXPECTED.

ED PALETTE OF BLACK AND WHITE

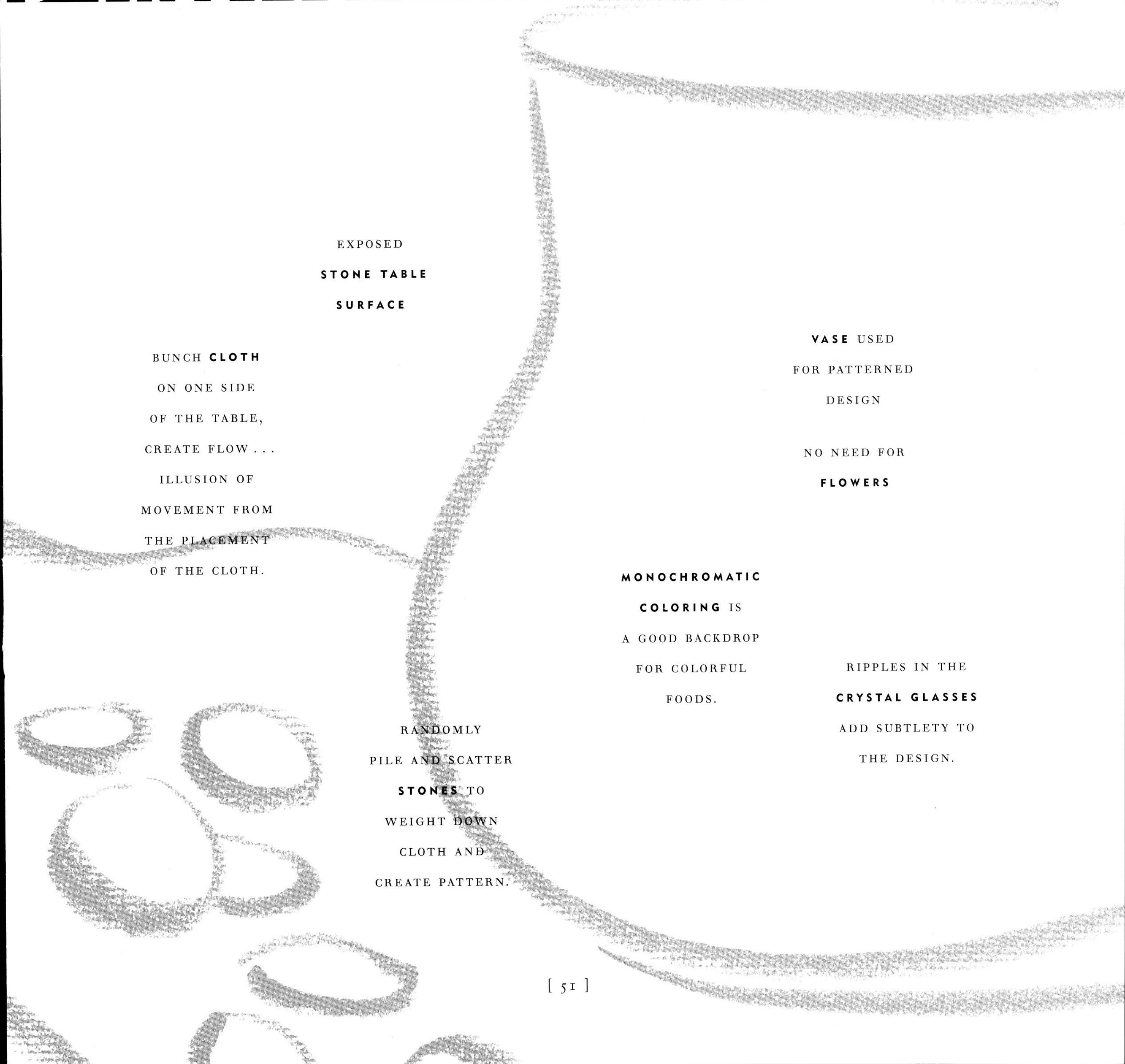

EXPOSED **STONE TABLE SURFACE**

BUNCH **CLOTH** ON ONE SIDE OF THE TABLE, CREATE FLOW . . . ILLUSION OF MOVEMENT FROM THE PLACEMENT OF THE CLOTH.

VASE USED FOR PATTERNED DESIGN

NO NEED FOR **FLOWERS**

MONOCHROMATIC COLORING IS A GOOD BACKDROP FOR COLORFUL FOODS.

RIPPLES IN THE **CRYSTAL GLASSES** ADD SUBTLETY TO THE DESIGN.

RANDOMLY PILE AND SCATTER **STONES** TO WEIGHT DOWN CLOTH AND CREATE PATTERN.

CREATING A PATTERNED SURFACE
BY LAYERING TRANSLUCENT MATERIAL

suggested menu: HEARTY FRENCH CASSOULET COMPOSED OF DUCK, SAUSAGES,
AND SLABS OF BACON SERVED OVER WHITE BEANS

FRISÉ SALAD TOPPED WITH HOMEMADE CROUTONS RUBBED WITH FRESH GARLIC

or

A DARK RISOTTO MADE WITH BLACK RICE, TOPPED WITH FRESH MUSSELS AND BABY CLAMS

BLACK CURRANT SORBET

ELEMENTS

STONE TABLE SURFACE

DRIED MAGNOLIA LEAVES

SILVER-COLORED
METALLIC WOVEN FABRIC

OVERSIZED GLASS
DINNER PLATES

HAND-GLAZED
CERAMIC CUPS

PEWTER SERVING BOWL

HEAVY-WEIGHT LINEN
NAPKINS

CUTLERY WITH
WOODEN HANDLES

CREATE A PATTERN BY ARRANGING LEAVES RANDOMLY ON THE STONE TABLE SURFACE. LAY METALLIC FABRIC OVER THE LEAVES AS SMOOTHLY AS POSSIBLE. OBJECTS ON THE TABLE WILL HOLD THE LEAVES IN PLACE.

HEAVY GLASS PLATES WEIGHT DOWN CLOTH AND LEAVES.

RANDOM PLACEMENT OF LEAVES CREATES MOVEMENT.

KEEP **SURFACE ELEMENTS** SIMPLE...LET LEAVES DOMINATE THE TABLE DESIGN.

FRUIT AND OTHER NATURAL MATERIALS PLACED DIRECTLY ON THE CLOTH BECOME PART OF THE PATTERN...ACCENT COLORS.

NEUTRAL COLORS ARE AN ELEGANT BACKDROP FOR RICHLY COLORED FOODS.

MANY **ELEMENTS**
ARE TRANSLU-
CENT...CLOTH
...LEAVES...
PLATES...STONE
SURFACE SHOWS
THROUGH...
ADDS DIMENSION.

BRUSH STROKE PATTERN ON CUPS

METALLIC FABRIC IS WOVEN FROM SILVER-AND-BLACK-COLORED THREADS... ELEGANT.

WARM GRAY-COLORED NATURAL LINEN NAPKINS... REFINED BUT EARTHY

NO NEED TO FINISH THE **EDGES** OF THE CLOTH.

GRAY-COLORED CLOTH OVER BEIGE-COLORED LEAVES MAKES A MONOCHROMATIC, WARM GRAY COLORING.

PEWTER FRUIT BOWL ADDS ELE-GANT METALLIC ACCENT.

DRIED MAGNOLIA LEAVES FROM FLORAL SUPPLY OR CRAFT STORE

[57]

CREATING RANDOM PATTERNS USING
PAINT AND NATURAL MATERIALS

suggested menu: A MIXTURE OF WINTER GREENS LIKE KALE, SWISS CHARD, AND BEET
GREENS SAUTÉED WITH LEEKS AND CHUNKS OF SWEET ITALIAN SAUSAGE OVER FETTUCCINE

WARM CRUSTY FRENCH BAGUETTE WITH GARLIC BUTTER

or

GRILLED WHITEFISH WITH A GREEN PARSLEY SAUCE SERVED WITH
FRESH ANGEL HAIR PASTA TOSSED WITH LEMON ZEST AND OLIVE OIL AND GARNISHED
WITH CHOPPED BASIL LEAVES AND GRATED PARMESAN CHEESE

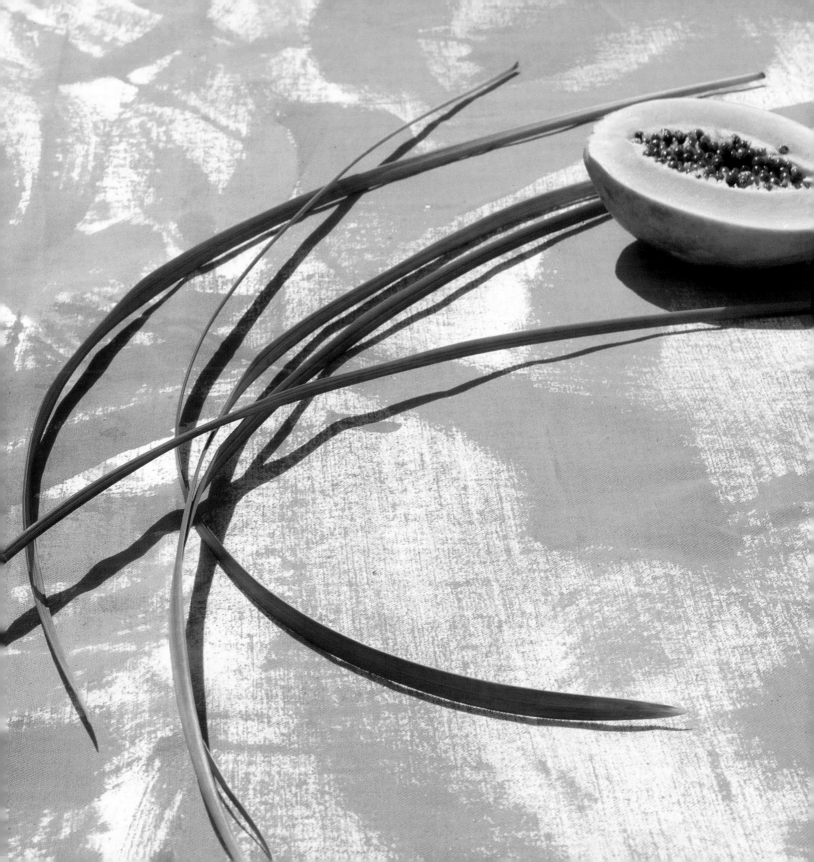

ELEMENTS

WOOD TABLE SURFACE

HAND-PAINTED
NATURAL CANVAS

BEAR GRASSES

LARGE HAND-CARVED
WOODEN BOWL FILLED
WITH FRUIT

PARCHMENT-COLORED
CERAMIC PLATES

SMALLER HAND-GLAZED
GREEN PLATES

GREEN GLASSES

HEAVY-WEIGHT
SILVER CUTLERY

KIWI-COLORED
COTTON NAPKINS

FRUITS ARE
ORGANIC TABLE
ORNAMENTS—
EDIBLE.

**ORANGES &
PERSIMMONS**
ON ORANGE-
PAINTED CLOTH—
COLOR ON COLOR—
CREATING RANDOM
PATTERN WITH
DIFFERENT SHAPES
AND HUES

**BEAR GRASSES
AND FRUITS**
RANDOMLY SCAT-
TERED CREATE
A PATTERN ON
THE CLOTH.

EXPOSE **WOODEN SURFACE** ON ONE END OF TABLE. GIVES
TABLE DESIGN A DIMENSION, MAKES PAINTED CLOTH A FOCAL POINT.

HAND-GLAZED PLATES HAVE SEVERAL SHADES OF COLORED
GLAZE "RUBBED" INTO SURFACE . . . NOT FLAT COLOR.

MIXING TWO KINDS OF **SOLID-COLORED CERAMICS** ADDS
INTEREST AND TEXTURE WITHOUT TOO MUCH DESIGN. HEAVY, CRUDE
CERAMIC NEEDED TO BALANCE BOLD ABSTRACT DESIGN OF CLOTH.

BRUSH STROKES ARE "LEAF"-SHAPED, ORGANIC... NOT RIGID.

SLIGHTLY GRAY-ING ORANGE-COLORED PAINT KEEPS COLOR "SOFT"...NOT TOO STRONG...BETTER WITH ORGANIC MATERIALS.

USE GENEROUS **NAPKINS AND CUTLERY.** SCALE STANDS UP TO PAINTED CLOTH AND FRUIT BOWL.

HAND-PAINTED CANVAS BECOMES FOCUS OF THE TABLE—THE STRONG DESIGN ELEMENT.

USE **PAINTED CLOTH** AS PIECE OF DECORATIVE ART, NOT AS TABLECLOTH.

LEAVE **EDGE OF CANVAS** UNFINISHED.

painting notes: WATER DOWN ACRYLIC PAINT TO THE CONSISTENCY OF HEAVY CREAM. USE A FIRM-BRISTLE 1½-INCH-WIDE BRUSH. STROKE CANVAS WITH ORGANIC LEAFY SHAPES. OVERLAP STROKES, BUT DON'T COVER TOO MUCH OF THE CLOTH. LET SOME OF THE NATURAL CANVAS COLOR AND TEXTURE SHOW THROUGH.

COMBINING TRADITIONAL AND CONTEMPORARY
PATTERNS IN A MODERN SETTING

suggested menu: FETTUCCINE WITH A LEMON ZEST CREAM SAUCE
SPRINKLED WITH TINY FRESH BASIL LEAVES
or
GREEK LEMON SOUP, FOLLOWED BY GRILLED FRESH SARDINES
SERVED WITH LOTS OF LEMON WEDGES

ELEMENTS

GALVANIZED-STEEL
TABLE SURFACE

ASSORTED PIECES OF
ANTIQUE STAFFORDSHIRE
POTTERY

HANDMADE JAPANESE
PORCELAIN PLATES

EARLY 19TH-CENTURY
AMERICAN REPRODUCTION
HANDBLOWN BOWL

BLUE-AND-WHITE
TEXTURAL NAPKINS

STERLING SILVER
FLATWARE

ASSORTED GREEN
AND YELLOW FRUITS

YELLOW AND GREEN COLORS OF FRUIT
ACT AS STRONG ACCENT COLORS FOR BLUE AND WHITE.

KEEP **TABLE DESIGN** SIMPLE...FOCUS ON THE PATTERN.

KEEP **ARRANGEMENT** SPONTANEOUS...INFORMAL.

MIX AS MANY VARYING **BLUE AND WHITE PATTERNS** AS POSSIBLE...
KEEP SETTING CALM...SERENE...ELEGANT.

KEEP **SHADES OF BLUE** SIMILAR.

ENGLISH STAFFORDSHIRE CERAMICS HAVE VARYING
DENSITIES OF PATTERNS AND SHADES OF BLUE.

STERLING FLATWARE IS ELEGANT...STANDS UP
TO FORMALITY OF ANTIQUES.

HANDMADE JAPANESE PLATES...SIMPLE DOT PATTERN
IS NAIVE, BUT PLATE IS VERY SOPHISTICATED.

HANDBLOWN GLASS ADDS MORE PATTERN IN A DIFFERENT MEDIUM... PATTERNED CERAMICS ONLY WOULD BE BORING.

STACK **TEXTURED NAPKINS** (SUBTLE TEXTURE IS MORE INTERESTING THAN SOLID BLUE). PATTERNED NAP-KINS WOULD BE TOO MUCH DESIGN, TAKE FOCUS AWAY FROM CERAMICS.

SLICK **CONTEMPO-RARY COMBINED WITH ANTIQUES** ...INTERESTING CONTRASTS... CLASSICAL **BLUE-AND-WHITE PAT-TERN** TIES WHOLE IDEA TOGETHER.

BOWL... **PLATTER**... PATTERNS BECOME ALMOST TEXTURAL.

FRUIT BECOMES AN ORGANIC SCULPTURAL ELEMENT— SCATTER AROUND TABLE.

BARE METAL TABLE SURFACE REFLECTS OBJECTS ON TABLE, ADDS DEPTH.

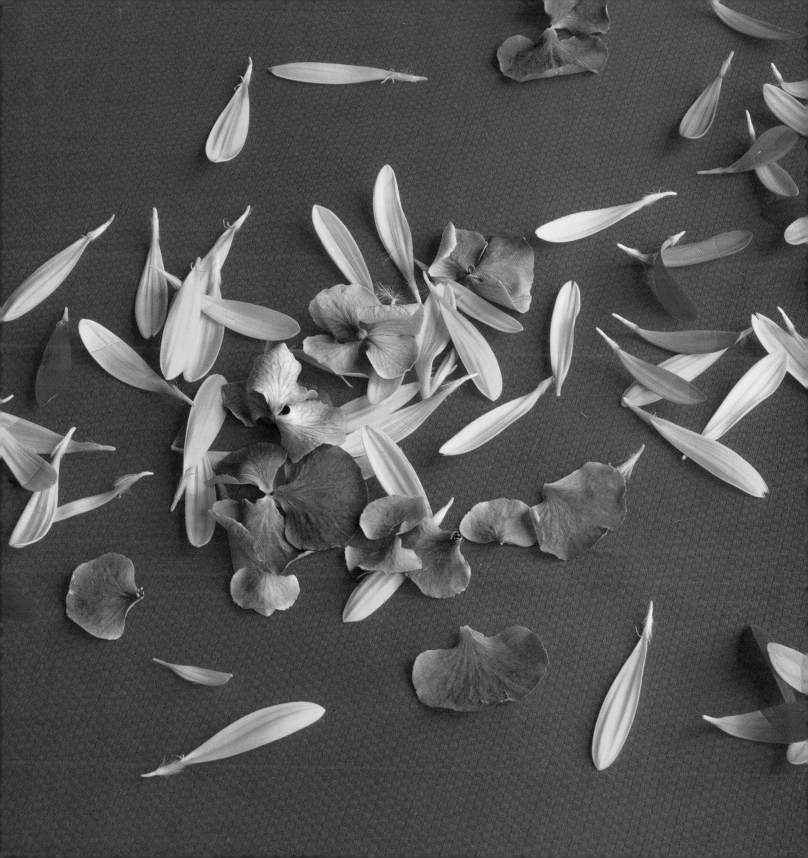

MIXING MULTIPLE PATTERNS FROM
A VARIETY OF SOURCES

suggested menu: BRAISED MOROCCAN LAMB SHANKS OVER YELLOW
COUSCOUS SCENTED WITH ORANGE FLOWER WATER SERVED WITH PRESERVED LEMONS
MULTICOLORED OVEN-ROASTED VEGETABLES LIKE BABY CARROTS, BRUSSELS SPROUTS, AND SMALL RED ONIONS
or
FRENCH TOAST MADE FROM THICK SLICES OF CHALLAH OR PANETTONE BREAD SERVED WITH GENEROUS
SLICES OF FRESH MELON AND BERRIES, DOLLOPED WITH YOGURT AND DRIZZLED WITH HONEY

ELEMENTS

RED COTTON PIQUÉ FABRIC

ETHNIC BLACK-AND-YELLOW
PRINTED FLOORCLOTHS

BLACK MEXICAN
POTTERY URN FILLED WITH
ASSORTED FLOWERS

HAND-GLAZED BLUE-
AND-WHITE PLATES

SQUARE GREEN PLATES

HAND-CARVED WOODEN
FRUIT BOWL

BLUE-AND-WHITE WOVEN
CHECK NAPKINS

STERLING SILVER
FLATWARE

DESIGN OF TABLE IS A PATTERN.

PATTERN = MOVEMENT.

COMBINE **THE PATTERNS** OF DIFFERENT OBJECTS.

MIX AS MANY PATTERNS AS POSSIBLE.

USING BLACK TONES DOWN AND BALANCES BRIGHT COLORS.

CREATE A PATTERN USING A MIXTURE OF TIGHTLY GATHERED FLOWERS.

THE COLORS AND TEXTURES OF THE INFORMAL **CLUSTER OF FLOWERS**
ADDS ANOTHER PATTERN . . . A STRONG FOCAL POINT.

GERBER DAISIES   LILACS   DAHLIAS   HYDRANGEAS

LAYER **PATTERNS**
ON THE RED
CLOTH TO "BUILD"
THE TABLE DESIGN.

OBJECTS ON TABLE CREATE PATTERNS ON RED CLOTH . . . THE "NEGATIVE SPACE" ON CLOTH BECOMES IMPORTANT.

INEXPENSIVE, CRUDELY PRINTED FLOORCLOTHS ADD BOLD, OVER-SCALED PATTERN.

SQUARE JAPANESE PLATES HAVE A WOVEN PATTERN PRESSED INTO THE GLAZE.

LAYER **FLOOR-CLOTHS** ON ONE END OF THE TABLE — KEEP ACTUAL DINING AREA ON RED FABRIC.

NAIVE WOVEN CHECK NAPKIN . . . UNEXPECTED COMBINATION . . . ADDS PATTERN IN WOVEN FORM.

FOOD ON THE PLATES BECOMES AN ELEMENT OF PATTERN.

MIX **SHAPES, SCALES, AND COLORS** OF PLATES.

USING LIVING ELEMENTS TO
ENLIVEN AN AUSTERE SETTING

suggested menu: WHOLE ROASTED FISH LIKE SALMON OR SEA BASS
GENEROUSLY GARNISHED WITH FRESH HERBS

FRESH FAVA BEANS MASHED AND SAUTÉED WITH GARLIC AND OLIVE OIL,
THEN SPREAD OVER WEDGES OF GRILLED TUSCAN BREAD, SERVED WITH A SIMPLE
SALAD OF FRESH ARUGULA LEAVES TOSSED WITH LEMON AND OLIVE OIL

or

INDIVIDUAL PIZZAS CAREFULLY PATTERNED WITH GRILLED VEGETABLES, OLIVES,
FRESH MOZZARELLA OR GOAT CHEESE AND THEN DRIZZLED WITH OLIVE OIL

ELEMENTS

NATURAL-COLORED CANVAS

OVERSIZED PORCELAIN
DINNER PLATES

NATURAL-COLORED
COTTON NAPKINS

OVERSIZED STAINLESS
FLATWARE

ASSORTED FRUITS, GOURDS,
AND VEGETABLES

**OFF-WHITE-
COLORED PLATES**
"FALL AWAY"
ONTO CANVAS.

ARTIST'S PAINTING CANVAS MAKES A TOTALLY NEUTRAL BACKDROP.

COTTON NAPKIN COLOR MATCHES CANVAS COLOR.

KEEP **TABLE DESIGN** SIMPLE, FOCUS ON COLOR AND PATTERN.

MIX **COLOR, SCALE, AND TEXTURES** OF NATURAL ELEMENTS.

SELECT **FRUITS AND VEGETABLES** SPECIFICALLY FOR THEIR COLOR AND PATTERN. THEY ARE THE ONLY DESIGN ELEMENTS ON THE TABLE.

FRUITS AND VEGETABLES SIT DIRECTLY ON THE CANVAS TABLE SURFACE.

OPEN AND BEND BACK **RADICCHIO LEAVES**— RESEMBLES A LARGE VIVIDLY PATTERNED FLOWER.

KEEP **PLACE SETTINGS** IN A RIGID ARRANGE- MENT...SCATTER FRUITS AND VEGETABLES RANDOMLY ACROSS THE TABLE... IN AND OUT OF PLACE SETTINGS.

OPEN SOME OF THE **BEAN PODS**... A SCATTERING OF FUCHSIA AND IVORY PATTERN.

RADICCHIO

PATTYPAN SQUASHES

SUGAR BABY WATERMELON

GARLIC

SMALL EGGPLANTS

ASSORTED GOURDS

PUMPKIN

CRANBERRY BEANS

AS CHILDREN WE ENCOUNTER OUR SURROUNDINGS DIRECTLY THROUGH OUR SENSES. WE LONG TO SEE, TASTE, AND TOUCH EVERYTHING. REMEMBER TRAILING YOUR FINGERS ALONG THE POLES OF A RUSTY FENCE, OR A CHALKY BRICK WALL, OR THE SCRATCHY BARK OF A GNARLED TREE? OR THE ALLURE OF WALKING BAREFOOT ON THE GRASS OR IN THE WARM, POWDERY SAND? TEXTURES STILL ENTICE AND INTRIGUE US; THEY STIR THE DESIRE TO CRUMBLE AND

stroke and hold things in our hands—to share in the organic, evolving process of all matter. In many ways, texture is a simple element because we can make an obvious physical connection to it. Yet, like the feeling of a soft blanket against our cheek that recalls us to the secure world of early childhood, the sensation of touch evokes meaning beyond the immediate. Textures excite our sensuous nature, which has its roots in our tactile memory of the past.

Much of the process of playing with texture on a table involves recognizing the impulse to touch things, and relishing the pull of that impulse. Texture provides spice to whet the appetite of the senses, firing a child-like curiosity about each element in any still life or on

any table. A pitted clay pot, a spiked branch of aromatic rosemary, crystallized ginger, seeded bread or crumpled linen—any of these irregular surfaces might attract or beguile us, or even churn up unanticipated or buried sensations. When we select textured elements for a table, Donna and I look for odd, imperfect materials—weathered objects; or natural matter not far removed from its origins; or unconventional raw ingredients—as well as more common textured materials with traditional applications such as lace or burlap or paper or frosted glass. Then we try to jangle the senses, to heighten our awareness of the substance and character of each component by combining unusual or contradictory textures in one setting—hard, reflective metals such as copper and stainless steel with the intricate weave of delicate lace; or silky precious fabrics with crude stone; or earthy, jagged, uneven textural surfaces with glossy objects made of glass or polished ceramics. By jangling the senses, we mean using the inherent physical nature of texture to visually wake us up, to alert us to the sensual complexity of the matter around us. Like sprinkling salt on melon to intensify the sweet taste of the fruit, mixing textural extremes often highlights the evocative essence of each.

As adults we do not necessarily need to touch a material for our senses to react. Just as we anticipate the taste of certain foods guided by what we see and smell, often merely the sight of a textured surface evokes remembered sensation, fueled by our imagination. Textures delight us and stir our passions. We experience a familiar connection with them, or feel comforted by them—or stimulated or fascinated by their intriguing composition. Our impulse to stroke the silky coat of a puppy, or to wrap ourselves in a fluffy blanket, anticipates the pleasurable sensation of softness that has charmed and soothed us in the past. Artists often exploit this evocative power of texture and turn it on its ear—to provoke or shock. One of the Surrealists, Meret Oppenheim, created a notorious still life in the 1930s of a cup, saucer, and spoon—mundane objects unexceptional in size or design except that the artist dressed them in an abundant covering of plush fur. The fur-covered cup was Oppenheim's attempt to annihilate our conventional conditioned response to an ordinary inanimate object, transforming it with texture into a suggestive fetish with disturbing intimate connotations. Another Surrealist, the Mexican artist Frida Kahlo, elevates a traditional still life of three pears on a plate to an erotically charged vision by embellishing the surface of ordinary fruit with strange textures that conjure up gruesome associations. Kahlo skillfully manipulates layers of lurid-colored oil paint on sheet metal until the prickly pears look bruised and bleeding, like damaged organic forms. These crude textures, reminiscent of Mexican *retablos*, the primitive church paintings created on rusted metal or scarred wood, enrich many of Kahlo's fantastic, magical paintings, and enhance both the expressive and the autobiographical content of her imagery. For Kahlo, texture intensifies emotion, serving both as a tool for altering perceptions, and a bridge between her cultural past and the world of her imagination.

A few weeks ago I visited a remote stretch of beach with a small group of friends—a deserted shore, patterned by thousands of extraordinary flat stones, shimmering with gemlike textures. The impression of textural opulence, glittering in the low sunlight of a late summer afternoon, reminded me of a tiled floor in a Byzantine palace—coral and black stones burnished with shiny mica; broken hunks of rose quartz, smooth on one side and glossy on the other; sandy stones of rusted red matte; marbled and ribbed fossilized shells with textured pockmarks; glassy tiny pebbles forming a mosaic on the sand; and coral and white speckled stones, their patina polished by the sea like shells of an exotic egg. Woven throughout this panorama of primitive forms was tactile evidence of the matter from the sea itself—gummy ropes of glistening green seaweed, and weathered wooden planks with gouges and splits containing clumps of brittle, dusty dried grasses. Many of the textured stones, in particular some translucent white stones with a chalky, frosted surface, moved me deeply—their powerful, enduring beauty suggested the passage of time

and the transformative effects of natural organic process.

Several of my friends showed me stones whose unique texture intrigued them, and we spontaneously began to discuss what their textures reminded us of. One friend, a visitor from northern Europe, thought that the irregular white rocks, which had fascinated me, looked like chunks of glacial snow or crystallized pieces of melting ice. Our conversation drifted to his memory about the coast of Norway and the landscape of his childhood. Another friend collected an amber stone, the size of a potato, with a matte texture created by years of pummeling and tumbling at the bottom of the sea. As he fingered the stone, and rubbed the dull surface against the back of his hand, he told me it made him hungry—it reminded him of cake batter, a bland sweet dough he tasted as a boy in his mother's kitchen. Texture makes us profoundly aware of the substance of all matter, which in turn awakens our sensuous nature and our sensory history—the formative tactile, physical experiences at the core of our needs and desires.

For artists, texture can be the stuff of dreams, the sacred glitter that adds emotional, even spiritual intensity to their work. The Viennese artist Gustav Klimt applied layers of textured gold leaf to many of his paintings and melancholy portraits, transporting them with an ornamental richness into a mesmerizing world of ephemeral passion and desire. That Klimt, the child of a goldsmith, created a transcendent world of dream-like illusion using the metallic textures that surrounded him as a child is unsurprising. For children, textured materials invite fantasy—they joyfully plunge their fingers into colored paint, and streak the vivid colors in striated ribbons across a blank page. They make mud pies, relishing the pliant, moist texture of the damp earth between their hands. I remember a game from my childhood—someone would be blindfolded, then made to hold various substances and guess what they were. In this game, which I now realize was a fairly sophisticated exercise about our conditioned sensory responses to texture, we limited ourselves to exploring materials through the sensations of touch, smell, and taste. The textures triggered our impressionable imagi-nations—they stirred up primal memory, and strange connections—that was the thrill. In our mind's eye, the bud from a cherry tree transformed into an exotic bug; the jagged shell of a pineapple became a scary animal. These childish responses to evocative objects mirror the way we continue to perceive textures—through the filter of our early sensory associations.

As you begin to experiment with texture, remember that child's game. Assemble a bunch of arresting tactile elements for a table—a piece of frosted glass; a few rough-skinned kiwis or downy apricots; a bunch of dried leaves; a rusted tin plate; or some crushed or pressed paper. With your eyes closed, select one object and explore it with your hands. Stroke the textured surface. Let your imagination go. Remember that texture, like taste, excites the senses the more you savor it. I have read that the Japanese have an aesthetic concept origi-nating with the tea ceremony called *wabi sabi*—the beauty of imperfect, unconventional, incomplete things. An aspect of the concept is simplicity, to pare down to the essence, but not to remove the poetry. Think about texture as the poetry of all matter—the irregular, imper-fect surface that speaks to us through our senses about the enduring substance within.

CONTRASTING REFINED CERAMIC
AND SILK WITH ROUGH STONE

suggested menu: ROASTED GARLIC SOUP DRIZZLED WITH AN HERB-INFUSED ROSEMARY
OIL AND SERVED WITH ASSORTED BREADS, HEARTY CHEESES, AND FRESH FRUIT

or

BAKED RICOTTA AND SPINACH TART SERVED WITH
ROASTED ROOT VEGETABLES LIKE CARROTS, BEETS, AND ONIONS

ELEMENTS

STONE TABLE SURFACE

WOVEN SILK SHAWLS

SLAB OF FLAGSTONE

CRACKLE-GLAZED
GREEN PLATES

MULTICOLORED
GLASSES

PURPLE TAFFETA
NAPKINS

PEARL-HANDLED
SILVER CUTLERY

A BROKEN PIECE OF **PATIO FLAGSTONE** BECOMES A SERVING PIECE FOR FOOD—AN ELEVATED TEXTURAL FOCAL POINT.

EXPOSE **STONE TABLE SURFACE.**

EXPOSE **BROKEN EDGE OF STONE**...LAYERS OF STONE ON STONE.

SERVE **BREADS AND CHEESE** DIRECTLY ON STONE SURFACE... DRY-TEXTURED CHEESE CRUMBLES NICELY.

JAPANESE CRACKLE-GLAZED DINNER PLATES ADD STRONG COLOR AND INTERESTING GLAZE TEXTURE...ADD ELEGANCE... DESIGN DOESN'T DETRACT FROM SHAWLS.

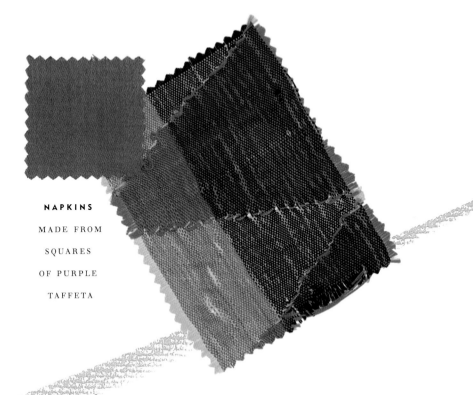

NAPKINS
MADE FROM
SQUARES
OF PURPLE
TAFFETA

TEXTURE OF **MULTICOLORED** **GLASSES** IS SIMILAR TO THE "WOVEN" QUALITY OF THE SHAWLS.

INEXPENSIVE **WOVEN SHAWLS** FROM AN ETHNIC CRAFT STORE — LAYER SHAWLS IN VARIOUS DIREC- TIONS, LEAVING AREAS OF THE STONE SURFACE EXPOSED.

LEAVE **TARNISH** ON SILVER CUTLERY — SOFT PATINA.

SCATTER **GREEN APPLES AND PLUMS** AROUND THE TABLE . . . VARYING SCALES AND TEXTURES WITH SIMILAR COLOR AND SHAPE MAKES AN INTER- ESTING COMBINA- TION BUT KEEPS COLOR LIMITED . . . FOCUS ON THE MULTICOLORED SHAWLS.

ALL ELEMENTS ARE STRONGLY COLORFUL — BUT NOT IN A "CUTE" WAY.

STRONG GREEN COLOR OF FRUIT AND PLATES SEEMS ALMOST EXAGGERATED ON GRAY STONE.

USING TRADITIONAL LACE

WITH GALVANIZED STEEL AND COPPER

suggested menu: SMALL ROASTED GAME BIRDS LIKE QUAIL OR SQUAB, STUFFED WITH SAUSAGE,

CHESTNUTS, AND FRESH HERBS, SERVED WITH PUREED SWEET POTATOES AND SAUTÉED ENDIVE

RICH CHOCOLATE CAKE TOPPED WITH SMALL SLICES OF CANDIED ORANGE PEEL

ELEMENTS

GALVANIZED-STEEL
TABLE SURFACE

THREE YARDS OF LACE

COPPER MIXING BOWL

TUBEROSES

NATURAL LINEN NAPKINS

VANILLA-COLORED
GLAZED CERAMIC PLATES

WHITE CERAMIC CUPS

STERLING SILVER
FLATWARE

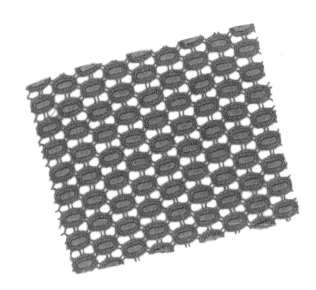

HEAVY-WEIGHT CAFÉ-AU-LAIT-COLORED LACE FROM A BRIDAL STORE...
UNFINISHED EDGES...WEIGHT OF LACE COMPLEMENTS WEIGHT
OF CERAMICS...NOTHING TOO DELICATE...BUT STILL VERY ELEGANT.

REFLECTIVE HARD SURFACE OF METAL IS AN INTERESTING
TEXTURAL CONTRAST TO THE SOFT LACE.

NEUTRAL COLORS WITH ACCENTS OF METAL...ELEGANT ENVIRONMENT

GALVANIZED STEEL HAS A SOFT PATINA...GRAY COLOR.

LARGE COPPER MIXING BOWL SITS AT ONE END OF
THE TABLE...LEAVE TARNISH...SOFTENS THE COLOR OF
THE METAL...ANOTHER TEXTURAL ELEMENT.

"SHAWL-LIKE"
ARRANGEMENT
OF LACE...
DRAPED OVER
REFLECTIVE METAL
SURFACE...
NOT FLAT...

PLATES ARE
PLACED ON ONE
SIDE OF THE
TABLE...LACE
BECOMES A
DESIGN ELEMENT,
NOT A TRADI-
TIONAL TABLE
COVERING.

PLACEMENT
OF PLATES
HAS A FLOW...
NOT RIGID.

LINEN NAPKINS
MATCH CERAMIC
COLOR...THEY
DON'T STAND OUT
OR COMPETE WITH
OTHER ELEMENTS.

BREAK OFF
LONG STEMS
OF FRAGRANT
TUBEROSES...
LAY FLOWERS IN
LARGE COPPER
BOWL...LET
FLOWERS DRAPE
OUT ONE SIDE...
ROMANTIC...
NOT TOO FUSSY
OR ARRANGED.

HEAVY-WEIGHT
JAPANESE CERAMIC
PLATES HAVE A
SPECKLED GLAZE...
ADD TEXTURAL
INTEREST, BUT
SUBTLE.

WHITE
CERAMIC CUPS...
UNEXPECTED
ALTERNATIVE TO
STEMWARE

MIXING UNREFINED WOVEN MATERIALS
WITH NATURAL TEXTURAL ELEMENTS

suggested menu: ASSORTED SMOKED AND CURED FISH LIKE
SMOKED TROUT WITH HORSERADISH CREAM, GRAVLAX WITH MUSTARD
SAUCE AND FRESH DILL, AND FRESH HERRING IN VINAIGRETTE
or
CREAM LEEK AND POTATO SOUP GARNISHED WITH LOTS OF FRESH DILL

CHICKEN ROASTED WITH FRESH APRICOT AND SHAVINGS OF CANDIED GINGER

ELEMENTS

AQUA-COLORED BURLAP

SHEETS OF YELLOW
PAPER WEBBING

OVERSIZED PALE-YELLOW
AND GREEN-COLORED
DINNER PLATES

PALE-GREEN RESIN
BOWL FILLED WITH
WHITE CURRANTS

SMALL BAMBOO DISH
FILLED WITH KOSHER SALT

TEXTURED SILK NAPKINS

VASES FILLED WITH
BUNCHES OF DILL AND
WILDFLOWERS

RECTANGULAR WOVEN
TRAY WITH APRICOTS

CUTLERY WITH
WOODEN HANDLES

COVER ENTIRE TABLE WITH A **WIDE PIECE OF BURLAP.**

COTTON WEBBING FROM ART SUPPLY OR PAPER STORE

RANDOMLY LAY **WEBBING OVER BURLAP** . . . OVERLAPPING
WEBBING MAKES A STRONGER YELLOW COLOR.

YELLOW WEBBING TONES DOWN BRIGHT TURQUOISE COLOR . . .
CREATES A "THIRD" COLOR THAT IS MORE INTERESTING.

TEXTURED SILK NAPKINS ARE AN INTERESTING
CONTRAST TO INEXPENSIVE BURLAP.

FINER TEXTURES ARE EASIER TO MIX . . . THEY TEND
TO BE MORE ELEGANT.

LOOSELY LAYER
SHEETS OF
WEBBING OVER
BURLAP . . . LEAVE
BENDS AND FOLDS
IN WEBBING TO
CREATE "MOTION."

USE TEXTURES
FROM NATURAL
MATERIALS.

HAND-GLAZED
PLATES IN
A MIXTURE OF
COLORS

LARGE BUNCHES
OF **TEXTURAL**
FLOWERS ADD
COLOR AND
HEIGHT . . .
PLACE VASES AT
THE END OF
THE TABLE.

PEACH-COLORED
FRUIT AND
FLOWERS ARE
PRETTY ACCENTS
TO TURQUOISE
AND YELLOW.

KEEP COLORS
SUBTLE BUT
INTERESTING.

WOVEN TRAY
BREAKS UP TABLE
SURFACE WITH
MORE TEXTURE.

COMBINING MATERIALS WITH
ROUGH AND SMOOTH TEXTURES

suggested menu: DELICATE CAPPELLINI PASTA TOPPED
WITH CRÈME FRAÎCHE AND BLACK CAVIAR
or
SAUTÉED FILLET OF SOLE SERVED WITH GARLIC CUSTARD
or
RISOTTO WITH WHITE TRUFFLES, DRIZZLED WITH TRUFFLE OIL

ELEMENTS

LARGE, FLAT-WHITE
LINEN SHEET

WHITE CERAMIC BOWLS
AND PLATES

CERAMIC ART BOWL

LARGE FABRIC PILLOWS

JAPANESE
RICE PAPER LAMP

FROSTED-GLASS
VOTIVE CANDLES

CRYSTAL GOBLETS

WHITE LINEN NAPKINS

STERLING SILVER
FLATWARE

**TALL CHARTREUSE-
COLORED CRYSTAL
GOBLETS** ARE
A STRONG COLOR
ACCENT...USE
FOR WATER OR
WINE...THEIR
COLOR BECOMES
A FOCAL POINT.

**FROSTED-
GLASS VOTIVES**
RANDOMLY SCAT-
TERED AROUND
THE PLACE
SETTINGS—FALL
AWAY ONTO LINEN,
CREATE SMALL
SPOTS OF LIGHT.

**BLACK-AND-
WHITE FABRIC
PILLOWS** ARE A
STRONG ACCENT
TO TABLE DESIGN.

ORGANIC

FORM OF BOWLS

ADDS DESIGN

INTEREST . . .

SCULPTURAL.

100% LINEN

SHEET, WASHED

AND DRIED, BUT

UNIRONED . . .

CRINKLED TEX-

TURE OF CLOTH

IS SUBTLE BUT

ADDS DEPTH.

ART BOWL

USED AS A

SERVING PIECE

ISAMU NOGUCHI RICE PAPER LAMP—USE INSTEAD OF "CENTER-PIECE" AT END OF THE TABLE . . . ADDS A TALL, GLOWING LIGHT SOURCE.

USE A VERY **LOW-WATTAGE BULB**, 15 WATTS . . . KEEP LIGHT SOFT.

HARDNESS OF GLASS CONTRASTS WITH

SOFTNESS OF PAPER LAMP AND WRINKLED LINEN.

STARCH AND

IRON **WHITE**

LINEN NAPKINS . . .

SUBTLE CON-

TRAST TO TABLE

COVERING . . .

ROUGH / SMOOTH.

MONOCHROMATIC TABLE SETTINGS ARE ELEGANT

BACKDROPS FOR FOOD—USE COLOR AS AN ACCENT . . . ADD

INTEREST WITH ORGANIC FORMS . . . SUBTLE.

VANILLA-COLORED CERAMIC GLAZE IN BOTH MATTE

AND GLOSSY FINISHES—SUBTLE CONTRAST OF TEXTURE . . .

DINNER PLATES/MATTE SALAD PLATES/GLOSSY.

STERLING FLATWARE ADDS FORMALITY TO CERAMICS.

COMBINING MULTIPLE TEXTURES
FROM A VARIETY OF NATURAL SOURCES

suggested menu: CREAMY SOFT POLENTA TOPPED WITH A MIXTURE OF
WOODY-FLAVORED MUSHROOMS LIKE CHANTERELLES, MORELS, PORCINI, AND CREMINI
FRESH SPINACH SAUTÉED WITH GARLIC AND SPRINKLED WITH TOASTED PINE NUTS
WINTER FRUITS LIKE FRESH PEARS, DRIED APRICOTS, DATES, AND
FIGS POACHED IN A WHITE WINE SYRUP WITH WHOLE CINNAMON STICKS

ELEMENTS

LINEN JUTE FABRIC

MARBLED CERAMIC
DINNER PLATES

WOVEN LINEN TEA TOWELS

LARGE DRIED POD USED
AS A SERVING BOWL

CUTLERY WITH CARVED
BAKELITE HANDLES

BRANCHES OF WILD
BLACKBERRIES

BRANCHES OF UNRIPENED
POMEGRANATES

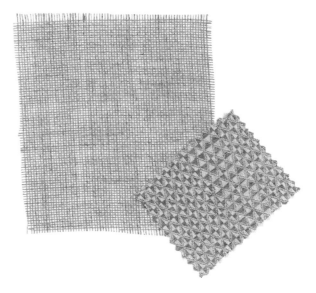

COVER ENTIRE TABLE WITH **JUTE,** SURFACE SLIGHTLY
EXPOSED THROUGH THE LOOSE WEAVE OF THE CLOTH . . . ADDS
AN INTERESTING DEPTH . . . TEXTURAL EFFECT.

NATURAL JUTE HAS A VERY GRAY COLOR CAST.

WOVEN LINEN HAND TOWELS MAKE GENEROUSLY SCALED NAPKINS.

KEEP **COLORS** SOFT, NEUTRAL, NATURAL, TONAL . . . EVEN THE FRUITS.

SIMPLE TABLE DESIGN . . . FOCUS INTEREST ON SUBTLE TEXTURES.

CHOOSE **OBJECTS** FOR THEIR TEXTURES . . . MIX SCALES OF TEXTURES.

EVERY **OBJECT** HAS A STRONG TEXTURAL EMPHASIS . . .
TIES TOGETHER SUBTLY.

LARGE HOLLOW **POD FROM PUERTO RICO—** A NATURAL SERVING BOWL

EARTHY-LOOKING **ORGANIC OBJECTS** CAN BE SOPHISTICATED.

BIND **BRANCHES OF POMEGRANATES** TOGETHER... SCATTER SOME LOOSELY AROUND TABLE.

SIMPLE TABLE DESIGN... FOCUS INTEREST ON SUBTLE TEXTURES.

KEEP **SERVING PIECES** MINIMAL.

LARGE-SCALE DINNER PLATES ...THE TEXTURAL BLEND OF THE MIXING CLAYS FORMS A PATTERN.

ANTIQUE **BAKE-LITE CUTLERY,** YELLOWED WITH AGE, ADDS ELEGANCE.

TWO COLORS OF CLAY ARE MIXED TOGETHER TO MAKE A "MARBLED EFFECT"... CLEAR GLAZE LETS THE COLOR OF THE CLAY SHOW THROUGH.

BUNCH OF **BLACKBERRY BRANCHES** MAKES AN EDIBLE BOUQUET...VERY TEXTURAL... PAINTERLY.

[115]

MIXING NATURAL TEXTURES,
PRIMARILY DERIVED FROM TREES

suggested menu: RICHLY SPICED AND COLORED CURRIED LAMB SERVED WITH A BROWN RICE PILAF

SMALL BOWLS FILLED WITH CONDIMENTS LIKE WHOLE TOASTED ALMONDS,
YELLOW RAISINS, AND CHUTNEY AND ASSORTED INDIAN BREADS LIKE PAPPADUM AND NAAN

or

SEAFOOD BAKED IN PARCHMENT PAPER WITH TINY BRANCHES OF FRESH OREGANO

ELEMENTS

BARK PAPER

PLACE MATS MADE
FROM BOUND TWIGS

ASSORTED COLORED PAPERS

MEXICAN TERRA-
COTTA BOWL

ROSEMARY SPRIGS

SWEDISH ANTIQUE
WOODEN CONTAINER

TUSCAN GREEN-GLAZED
STONEWARE BOWL

COCONUT-SHELL BOWL

POD BOWL

JAPANESE PLATES
AND RICE BOWLS

FINNISH WOODEN CUTLERY

USE **SWEDISH ANTIQUE CONTAINER** TO SERVE BREAD OR CRACKERS . . . THE RECTANGULAR SHAPE COMPLEMENTS THE OTHER OBJECTS ON THE TABLE.

HANDMADE BARK PAPER . . . AN INTERESTING TEXTURAL SURFACE . . . A GOOD BACKDROP FOR THE COLORS OF FOODS . . . TWO OR THREE SHEETS COVER THE TABLE SURFACE

SHEETS OF **ABSORBENT COLORED PAPER** ARE CUT INTO NAPKINS . . . TRY VARYING NAPKIN FOLDS AND SIZES . . . USE PAPER NAPKINS AS A COLOR ACCENT ON A NEUTRAL SETTING.

COLORS ARE MOSTLY NEUTRAL . . . COLOR FOCUS IS ON THE FOOD AND THE NAPKINS.

MIX OBJECTS
FROM MULTIPLE
ORIGINS.

STACK
TEXTURED
RICE BOWLS
AND PLATES.

ARRANGE
OBJECTS WITH
VARYING HEIGHTS
AND SCALES...
THE LARGER,
MORE DECORATIVE
OBJECTS WILL
ANCHOR THE
TABLE DESIGN.

STACK AND LAYER
COMPONENTS...
KEEP LAYOUT
ENGINEERED.

TWIG PLACE MAT
IS THE CENTER
OF THE TABLE...
ARRANGE AND
STACK ELEMENTS
AROUND IT.

VARYING SHAPES
AND SIZES OF
HAND-CARVED
WOODEN CUTLERY
FROM FINLAND

NATURAL
MATERIALS
ARRANGED IN A
RIGID SETTING
ARE AN INTEREST-
ING CONTRAST....
SCATTER SMALLER
OBJECTS LESS
RIGIDLY AROUND
LARGER ONES.

TEXTURAL,
WOODY, ROSE-
MARY SPRIGS ADD
BOTH COLOR AND
FRAGRANCE...
DECORATIVE
MEXICAN BOWL—
OFF-CENTER
PLACEMENT.

TEXTURED
GLAZES ON
CERAMICS ARE
SUBTLE BUT ADD
TO THE IDEA.

USE **DRIED**
PODS AND SHELLS
AS RECEPTACLES
FOR NUTS AND
CONDIMENTS.

MATE

MATERIALS ARE THE INGREDIENTS WE USE TO CREATE. WE SELECT MATERIALS TO LIVE AND WORK WITH EVERY DAY, FLAVORING OUR SURROUNDINGS WITH SUBTLE MESSAGES ABOUT OUR PREFERENCES AND OUR DESIRES. A TABLE OF BLEACHED, ROUGH PINE INSTEAD OF POLISHED MARBLE; A SLATE TERRACE INSTEAD OF MOSS-STAINED BRICK; BOWLS MADE OF GLASS AND GLEAMING STAINLESS STEEL RATHER THAN PAINTED CERAMIC AND TERRA-COTTA—THESE

casual choices about the matter we are drawn to also reflect complex aspects of our ingrained taste. Materials speak of private experience, of needs and longings—they call to us as distinctly as certain pieces of music do. Materials often possess us as much as we possess them.

Working with any material involves discovery of its essence, the unique core that we respond to and that generates our emotional attachment to it. Certain materials invite intimacy—those that are earthy or obviously shaped by the effects of time; objects with cracks or chips; or ancient wood tarnished by exposure to sun and rain. We want to hold these materials in our hands, and explore the history engraved in their textured surfaces. Other materials are ephemeral, momentary—

living things that will inevitably die, such as a peach or a rose; or fragile materials such as tissue or dry leaves. These materials usually affect me with a sense of urgency, the impulse to use them *now* before the seasons change or their glowing color fades. When Donna and I create a table, we search for materials that delight us, that make us want to touch them, to turn them inside out or upside down, to twist and bend them. We often combine humble materials, such as a weathered chunk of stone or a pile of mussel shells, with fine silk fabrics or a piece of antique silver, so that we bridge the gap between familiar, intimate elements, and materials that are spectacular but remote. Sometimes we restrict ourselves to only one material, such as glass, exploring transparency in all its configurations; or the grains, textures, and patterns of wood. Revealing the infinite variety of each material means we disclose its substance and heart, the essence of the material.

Materials inspire us to conceive ideas; they also provide a channel for our inspiration. When an artist transforms a basic, modest material—a piece of canvas or a hunk of clay—into a dazzling painting or a powerful sculpture, the work of art possesses infinitely more universal value than the material from which the art is created. But is that always the case? As the medium—the blank slate awaiting poetic language—ordinary canvas or clay has an intrinsic worth to the artist far greater than any tangible price that we can measure. We assess the value of any material—mass produced or unique, fine or rustic, traditional or unconventional, slick or crude—in proportion to our desire for it. Subversive artists, such as René Magritte and Salvador Dalí, have created still lifes that taunt us with this desire, and the emotional or symbolic importance we assign to the matter around us. In some of his paintings, Magritte intentionally renames the objects, identifying a leaf as a table, a pitcher as a piece of fruit, or a high-heeled shoe as the moon. His representation (or misrepresentation) of objects provokes us to examine our allegiance to any material that we covet—is the leaf more or less important as a table or as a leaf? Is the shoe more wonderful as the moon? Do we need it or crave it more or less? Magritte's challenge to us—to see any and all matter as an enigma, divorced of a banal identity—is an invitation to experiment, to nourish our own wishful fantasies or creative desires, to find stimulus in any material.

I have made many visits to the primitive regional markets in rural Mexico—places filled with mysterious and fantastic materials redolent of foreign aromas, exploding with vibrant colors—a theatrical spectacle of magical substances and objects. The materials, locally grown, woven, or sculpted, and often unidentifiable to my urban eyes, are layered like abstract sculpture in wild patterns and designs—beans, spices, fragile pottery, woven textiles, fruit, vegetables, a thousand varieties of chiles, chocolate, flowers, embroidered cloth, herbs, gourds, silver pitchers, and tin pots. I often photograph the elaborate arrangements of indigenous stuff—partly as an exercise in freeing my imagination; but mostly for the sheer visual joy of recording the extraordinary shapes, colors, and textures. The most enticing displays are still lifes made from poignantly simple materials— weathered wooden crates of different sizes, covered with flamboyant plastic sheets, and piled with yellow and green bananas; or low rectangular woven baskets perched on rusted tin counters, or on embroidered shawls brimming with ruby-colored plum tomatoes and sliced ginger-colored melons. Inside a market church, I photographed a classically composed still life made of primitive materials used pragmatically and imagina- tively—an ancient wooden table with a collection of fresh cantaloupes pierced with dozens of sticks deco- rated with colored flags made of metallic paper—in front of a frescoed plaster wall adorned with a pattern of primitive orange flowers painted in vegetable dyes. With unrestrained pageantry, the market vendors dis- play, sell, and employ all manner of materials—metal pipes, colored rope, baskets, bricks, flowers made of onion petals, and even giant radishes sculpted into bird and animal forms by local farmers.

These abundant markets crammed with exotic materials remind me that taste and desire are often defined by our unique cultural and personal experi- ences. Many esoteric materials entice me as I wander through the spice-filled tents in Mexico, even though I have no idea of their origin or their function. Twisted roots and textured gourds, strange dried herbs and can- died orchid bulbs draw me as some pieces of sculpture do; I want to own them, to put them on my favorite stone table so that I will see them as I work. Donna and I often explore alternate ways to use familiar materials on a table—placing a gnarled branch, like a twisted snake, down the length of a long wooden surface, or stacking a dozen breakable eggs in their perfect white shells in a clear glass vase. Use your imagination, as a sculptor might, to see the whimsical or bizarre nature of an ordinary, even mundane, object. For example, pre- tend for a few minutes that you did not know what an eggplant was. Would you try to cook it and eat it? Or would you be seduced by its dark rich color and its sen- suous shape? Hold one in your hands and feel its surface, as smooth as buffed leather. Place several eggplants on your favorite table, and notice how their purple hues mingle with polished wood or shiny metal. Dig out a chipped or cracked vase from the dark place you ban- ished it to, and feel its texture. Cracks and stains can be fascinating adornments, speaking to us about the pas- sage of time and the visible signs of a natural occurrence. They tend to make us immediately aware of the character of a material, its consistency and substance, its endurance and its fragility.

Looking beyond the surface of a material to its essence and its history begins the creative process. Translating ideas from one material to another—the fusion of organic forms and classical concepts—goes to the heart of making a work of art, especially still life and sculpture. The British artist Henry Moore, whose vision was deeply rooted in organic, natural materials, combed beaches collecting fragments of shells and pebbles; and he prowled the countryside near his home in Hertfordshire for bones and branches to serve as his inspiration. For one of his famous sculptures of an abstract standing figure, an animal shoulderblade that he discovered in a field literally became the physical model from which he created his final, enormous piece. Moore believed in letting the core properties of his material fuse into the art he was shaping—in his hands, the veins of a piece of stone seem to evolve into the veins of a human figure. As we look at the metamorphosis of Moore's universal stone forms, it does not seem surprising that he was the son of a coal miner—an artist who learned as a child about the primitive power of matter and the life force inherent in organic materials.

Every table you create begins with the materials, with one magical substance, whose essence—the chalky texture or simple patina or luscious color—draws you to it. As you would with any still life, build upon that distinctive quality layer by layer with a variety of materials, inventing intriguing relationships among the objects that you desire.

CREATE A SURFACE WITH SLATE TILES
AS A SETTING FOR ORGANIC MATERIALS

suggested menu: ASSORTED GARDEN-FRESH HEIRLOOM TOMATOES
DRIZZLED WITH OLIVE OIL AND SERVED WITH FRESH GOAT CHEESE

CORN ON THE COB BRUSHED WITH FRESH HERB BUTTER

GRILLED FRESH VEGETABLES OVER FETTUCCINE SPRINKLED WITH
CRUMBLED FETA CHEESE AND CHOPPED OLIVES
or
SIMPLY GRILLED FISH OR MEAT SERVED WITH GARDEN-FRESH
VEGETABLE RATATOUILLE AND CRUSTY PEASANT BREAD

CREATE A SURFACE WITH SLATE TILES

ELEMENTS

SQUARE SLATE
PATIO TILES

TERRA-COTTA PLATES
WITH CLEAR GLAZE

LARGE ANTIQUE
GLASS COFFEE JAR
FILLED WITH MARINATING
GOAT CHEESES

GREEN GLASS TUMBLERS

THICKLY WOVEN
GREEN COTTON NAPKINS

RUSTIC STAINLESS
FLATWARE

GREEN ITALIAN
CERAMIC BOWL

GRAPEVINES

ASSORTED GARDEN
VEGETABLES

VEGETABLE **COLORS** LOOK VERY RICH AGAINST SLATE-GRAY SURFACE.

LEAVE **TOMATOES** ON BRANCHES.

KEEP **MATERIALS** NATURAL IN FORM...KEEP **COLORS** PURE... MOST OF THE COLOR AND FOCUS IS ON THE VEGETABLES.

SCATTER OR ARRANGE **BEANS** IN INFORMAL PILES AROUND TABLE.

BOWLS OF **YELLOW PEAR TOMATOES**

NATURAL, CLEAR-GLAZED TERRA-COTTA **PLATES** REINFORCE GARDENLIKE FEEL WITH MATERIALS.

12"-SQUARE SLATE PATIO TILES, FITTED TOGETHER UNEVENLY TO CREATE THE TABLE SURFACE... THEIR ROUGH AND UNEVEN TEXTURE MAKES THEM MORE INTERESTING. (IF TILES HAVE BEEN OUTSIDE, BE SURE THEY HAVE BEEN SCRUBBED CLEAN AND DRIED BEFORE ASSEMBLING TABLE SURFACE.)

GOAT CHEESES MARINATING WITH BRANCHES OF THYME IN GOLDEN-COLORED OLIVE OIL... THE SCALE OF THE JAR BECOMES A FOCAL POINT... SERVE CHEESES DIRECTLY FROM THE JAR.

NATURAL ELEMENTS SCATTER AROUND PLACE SETTINGS AND ALONG THE CENTER OF THE TABLE... THE BRIGHT COLORS OF THE VEGETA-BLES BECOME THE FOCUS.

ROUGHLY TEXTURED CHARTREUSE-COLORED GLASS TUMBLERS... USE FOR WATER OR WINE... STRONG GREEN COLOR TIES INTO VINE AND NAPKIN COLOR.

HEAVY TEXTURE OF NAPKINS... SUBSTANTIAL... STANDS UP WELL TO OTHER MATERIALS ... COLOR TIES INTO GLASSES

LEAVE BUNCHES OF GRAPES AND NATURAL MATTER ATTACHED TO VINES. (BE SURE TO CHECK VINES FOR BUGS AND DEBRIS BEFORE PLACING THEM ON THE TILES.)

VINES STRETCH ACROSS SQUARE TILES... CREATE A FLOW, MOVE-MENT... BREAK GRID PATTERN.

USE OUTDOOR, GARDENLIKE MATERIALS TO MAKE A SOPHISTI-CATED SETTING INSIDE... KEEP MATERIALS NATURAL.

CREATING A MONOCHROMATIC TABLE
USING ALL NATURAL ELEMENTS

suggested menu: FRESH FIGS, WARM GOAT CHEESE, AND PANCETTA BACON SERVED OVER BITTER GREENS

PUMPKIN- AND SAGE-STUFFED RAVIOLI SERVED WITH WHOLE ROASTED RED AND ORANGE BEETS

FOCACCIA TOPPED WITH ONIONS AND ROSEMARY

ELEMENTS

STRIP OF WOVEN RAFFIA
WALL COVERING

LARGE NARROW
TREE BRANCH

WHITE ACORN SQUASHES

OVERSIZED PUTTY-COLORED
CERAMIC PLATES

SMALL CLEAR GLASSES

LINEN NAPKINS

TALL TEXTURED
PILLAR CANDLES

CUTLERY CARVED FROM
COCONUT SHELLS

PEWTER DISH

UNROLL **RAFFIA**
DOWN CENTER
OF TABLE.

METAL KEEPS
TABLE FROM
GETTING TOO
EARTHY.

SILVER ACCENT...
SOPHISTICATED
CARVED PEWTER
DISH FROM
BARCELONA JEWELRY
DESIGNER

LEAVE **FRAYED EDGE OF RAFFIA**...EXPOSE
WOODEN TABLE SURFACE ON BOTH SIDES OF RAFFIA.

OVERSIZED LINEN NAPKINS...LUXURIOUS

RESTRICTING COLORS PUTS MORE EMPHASIS ON THE MATERIALS
AND THE DESIGN OF THE TABLE.

NATURAL COLORS ARE A GOOD BACKDROP FOR JEWEL-TONED FOOD.

NATURAL MATERIALS IN AN ELEGANT SETTING

MAKE SURE
BRANCH IS
BRUSHED FREE
OF DIRT OR
DEBRIS BEFORE
PLACING IT ON
THE RAFFIA.

USE **SIMPLE**
GLASSES INSTEAD
OF TRADITIONAL
STEMWARE.

BRANCH LAID
DOWN CENTER
OF TABLE ESTAB-
LISHES PLACE-
MENT OF DINNER
PLATES ON
EITHER SIDE.

SCATTER A
RANDOM ARRANGE-
MENT OF GOURDS
ALONG BOTH SIDES
OF BRANCH.

PUTTY-COLORED
HAND-GLAZED
PLATES...
LARGE SCALE
GIVES IMPORTANCE
TO EACH PLACE
SETTING.

WHITE GOURDS
ARE ALMOST
GHOSTLIKE.

CANDLES
SIT DIRECTLY
ON TABLE.

USING ROUGH, PLAIN MATERIAL

TO CREATE AN ELEGANT TABLE

suggested menu: ASSORTED ANTIPASTO-TYPE FOODS LIKE SLICES OF CURED
MEATS (SALAMI OR PROSCIUTTO), EGGPLANT CAPONATA, BITE-SIZE
CHUNKS OF VARIOUS CHEESES, MARINATED FRESH ARTICHOKE HEARTS, AND
TOASTED BRUSCHETTA TOPPED WITH BLACK OLIVE AND ANCHOVY TAPENADE

ELEMENTS

STONE TABLE SURFACE

BURNT-ORANGE-COLORED
WOOL FELT

LARGE HAND-CARVED
WOODEN TRAY

WOODEN SERVING BOWL

LACQUERED
WOODEN PLATES

JAPANESE CERAMIC
TEACUPS

COTTON CANVAS
NAPKINS

BRANCHES

ASSORTED WOODEN
CUTLERY

**LARGE-SCALED
"EARTHY"-LOOK-
ING FRUITS** SUCH
AS PEARS AND
MANGOES ADD
STRONG COLOR
AND SHAPE . . .
SCULPTURAL . . .
NOT AT ALL TROP-
ICAL IN FEEL.

GOLD-COLORED
OVERSIZED **COT-
TON NAPKINS**—
SIMILAR TO THE
COLOR OF THE
WOODEN PLATES

THE COLORS
FROM THE WOOD,
FELT, AND FRUITS
ARE ALL WARM.

**STRONGLY
COLORED FELT**
FROM A CRAFT
STORE — LEAVE
UNFINISHED
EDGE — LAY FLAT
ACROSS THE STONE
SURFACE, DIVID-
ING THE TABLE
IN HALF.

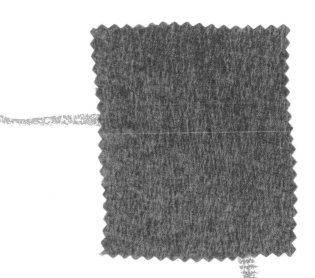

KEEP ALL
MATERIALS
ORGANIC,
"ROUGH-HEWN."

RESTRICT ALL
UTENSILS AND
RECEPTACLES TO
ONE MATERIAL...
BUT MIX SCALES
AND STYLES.

DIVIDE **TABLE SURFACE** IN HALF WITH FELT.

STONE AND FELT CONTRAST WITH EACH OTHER—HARD AND SOFT.

UNFINISHED MEXICAN WOODEN TRAY...PLACED OFF CENTER...
BREAKS THE STRONG LINE OF THE FELT.

BRANCHES CASUALLY LIE ACROSS TABLE...SOFTEN THE
STRONG VERTICAL LINE OF THE FELT.

NO SPECIFIC AREA FOR A **CENTERPIECE**...ENHANCES FLOW OF THE
SETTING...COMPOSE DESIGN AROUND LARGE TRAY AND BRANCHES.

LET **FRUITS**
SCATTER INFOR-
MALLY AROUND
LARGER OBJECTS.

CASUALLY PLACED OVERSIZED **NATURAL WOODEN BOWLS AND**
TRAYS...SCULPTURAL SERVING PIECES

STACK
WOODEN PLATES
AND UTENSILS
AT ONE END OF
THE TABLE.

STONE

FELT

MIXING MATERIALS ON A LOOSE
ARRANGEMENT OF CERAMIC TILES

suggested menu: SEAFOOD BOUILLABAISSE SCENTED WITH SAFFRON AND
FRESH FENNEL SERVED WITH MESCLUN SALAD AND LOAVES OF CRUSTY BREAD
or
SPAGHETTI SAUTÉED WITH GARLIC, PARSLEY, OLIVE OIL, AND CAPERS

ELEMENTS

BLUE-AND-GREEN
WOVEN FABRIC

GLAZED CERAMIC TILES

BLUE GLASS PLATES

GLAZED STONEWARE BOWLS

AQUA-COLORED GLASSES

OVERSIZED STAINLESS
FLATWARE

TALL CERAMIC FLOWERPOT

BUDDHA'S-HANDS CITRUS

ALASKAN CRAB CLAWS

GLASSES

MODERN GLASS PLATES AND GLASSES FROM FINLAND

MIX MATERIALS, BUT KEEP **COLORS** CONSISTENT...COOL...INTERESTING
MONOCHROMATIC BACKDROP FOR YELLOW LEMONS AND RED CLAWS.

HAND-GLAZED STONEWARE BOWLS FROM PROVENCE ADD
EARTHINESS...LARGE ENOUGH TO USE INSTEAD OF DINNER PLATES.

KEEP ARRANGEMENT OF **MATERIALS** LOOSE...NOT RIGID...
CREATE THE ILLUSION OF MOVEMENT.

IRREGULAR GLAZE ON TILES CREATES A "WATER-LIKE" FEELING ...MOVEMENT.

WOVEN FABRIC LOOSELY DRAPED ON ONE SIDE OF THE TABLE

LEMONS ARE EDIBLE PIECES OF SCULPTURE... INTERESTING ORGANIC FORMS... NOT JUST FOR DECORATION.

TWO COLORS WOVEN TOGETHER CREATE THE ILLU-SION OF A THIRD COLOR...MORE INTERESTING THAN FLATLY COLORED CLOTH.

ARRANGE **TILES** ON AND OFF CLOTH.

CLOTH IN SHADE SIMILAR TO THE TILES CREATES INTER-ESTING PLAY ON HARD AND SOFT.

SIT **FOOD** DIRECTLY ON TILES...GOOD FOR BOTH HOT AND COLD.

[149]

CREATING A TABLE PRIMARILY
USING CLEAR GLASS

suggested menu: OYSTERS ON THE HALF-SHELL
SERVED ON BEDS OF SEA SALT CRYSTALS WITH A MIGNONETTE SAUCE
or
FRESH SCALLOP CEVICHE SERVED INDIVIDUALLY ON THEIR SHELLS

CRACKERS, SMALL TOASTS, AND AN ASSORTMENT OF FLAVORED RUSSIAN VODKA

ELEMENTS

AQUA-COLORED SHEER
METALLIC FABRIC

OVERSIZED GLASS PLATES

ASSORTED SCALES
AND STYLES OF CRYSTAL
AND GLASS VASES

STACKED CRYSTAL
"CANDY DISHES" FILLED
WITH LARGE CRYSTALS
OF SEA SALT

AQUA-BLUE GLASS CARAFE

TALL GLASS VASE FILLED
WITH EGGS

CRYSTAL VODKA GLASSES

SMALL GLASS PLATE
STACKED WITH WHITE
OYSTER MUSHROOMS

TURQUOISE-COLORED
SILK NAPKINS

STERLING SILVER
CUTLERY

LIGHT EMPHA-SIZES THE BEAUTY AND TRANSLU-CENCY OF GLASS.

TURQUOISE OF FABRIC HAS A "WATERLIKE" FEEL.

METALLIC FABRIC "RIPPLES" AROUND OBJECTS... "FLOWS" DOWN TABLE SURFACE. (NO NEED TO HEM THE EDGES OF THE CLOTH.)

TURQUOISE-COLORED SILK NAPKINS MATCH THE COLOR OF THE METAL CLOTH... THEY BLEND, FALL AWAY.

USE **ELLIPTICAL CRYSTAL VASE** TO HOLD CRACKERS AND BREADS.

INEXPENSIVE HEAVY GLASS PLATES...OVER-SIZED SCALE ELEGANT FOR SERVING OYSTERS

KEEP **SETTING SIMPLE**... DREAMLIKE.

FREE-FORM ALVAR AALTO VASE FROM FINLAND... ART PIECE... CREATES A TALL FOCAL POINT.

GLASS PIECES RANGE IN SIZE AND SCALE... "LAYER" THEM... FILL SOME WITH FOOD... LEAVE SOME EMPTY.

USE **GLASS OBJECTS** TO CRE-ATE THE FEELING OF WATER... EMPHASIZE THE WATERLIKE QUALITY OF GLASS...FLUID.

CRYSTAL COMPOTE FILLED WITH EDIBLE SILVER-COATED CANDIED ALMONDS.

SERVE **CHILLED OYSTERS** ON ROCK SALT.

COMBINING FINE METALLIC MATERIAL
WITH CRUDE PAINTED CANVAS

suggested menu: SLIVERS OF AGED STILTON CHEESE, SLICED PEARS,
AND POMEGRANATE SEEDS SERVED OVER ASSORTED MIXED GREENS

GRILLED VEAL ROAST WRAPPED IN BACON AND CHARRED WITH BRANCHES
OF FRESH ROSEMARY SERVED WITH WARM PUMPKIN GRATIN

CRÈME BRÛLÉE

ELEMENTS

MOSSY-GREEN-COLORED
PAINTED CANVAS

SHEER GOLD-COLORED
METALLIC FABRIC

WHITE STAR
CALATHEA LEAVES

FINNISH TERRA-COTTA
BOWL FILLED WITH
BLOOD ORANGES

RED-GLAZED CERAMIC
PLATES WITH GOLD EDGE

TUSCAN TERRA-COTTA MUGS

MEXICAN TERRA-
COTTA BOWL

BURNT-ORANGE-
COLORED SILK SHANTUNG
NAPKINS

METALLIC FABRIC DRAPED OVER CANVAS, ON A DIAGONAL
ACROSS ENTIRE TABLE SURFACE. SLIGHTLY BUNCHED, NOT FLAT
OR STAGNANT...RIPPLES CREATE INTERESTING SHADOWS.

FABRIC WOVEN WITH METALLIC GOLD AND BLACK THREADS

HAND-PAINTED ARTIST'S CANVAS, BRUSHED WITH MOSSY-GREEN-
COLORED ACRYLIC PAINT. WATER DOWN PAINT TO THE CONSISTENCY
OF HEAVY CREAM...APPLY WITH A LARGE MEDIUM-BRISTLED
BRUSH...UNEVEN APPLICATION ADDS TO THE PATINA.

NO NEED TO HEM THE **EDGE** OF THE CANVAS.

SHEER FABRIC OVER HEAVY CANVAS IS AN INTERESTING
CONTRAST OF COLOR AND MATERIALS.

SLIGHT SHEEN OF **SILK SHANTUNG NAPKINS** WORKS
NICELY WITH METALLIC FABRIC.

NATURAL **ELEMENTS** SCAT-TERED AROUND THE TABLE GIVE THE DESIGN AN ORGANIC FEEL AND ADD COLOR.

UNDERSIDE OF LEAVES IS PUR-PLE. PLACE LARGE LEAVES AROUND TABLE SURFACE WITH UNDERSIDE FACING UP . . . EXOTIC COLORING WORKS WELL WITH THE GREEN.

NUTS, FIGS (TWO COLORS), **LEAVES, BLOOD ORANGES**

LARGE TERRA-COTTA VASE FROM FINLAND BECOMES A FOCAL POINT AT ONE END OF THE TABLE.

DEEP-RED PLATES HAVE A BURNISHED GOLD EDGE . . . GOLD ACCENT MAKES EARTHY MATERI-ALS SEEM MORE ELEGANT.

MIX **RED AND GREEN WITH ACCENTS OF PURPLE** . . . UNUSUAL COMBI-NATION MAKES A MORE INTEREST-ING DESIGN . . . EXOTIC . . . ELEGANT.

NATURAL TERRA-COTTA CERAMICS VARY IN COLOR DEPENDING ON THE CLAY AND THE ORIGIN . . . MIX SHADES . . . COM-BINE DIFFERENT TEXTURES.

TUSCAN CERAMIC MUGS . . . AN ALTERNATIVE TO WINEGLASSES.

TERRA-COTTA COLORS

SETTING THE TABLE IS A CHORE PERFORMED WITH LITTLE THOUGHT SEVERAL TIMES A DAY IN MOST HOMES, A TASK APPROACHED WITH ANXIETY, SOMETIMES EVEN DREAD, BY MANY HOSTS OBSESSED WITH GETTING EVERYTHING JUST RIGHT. IT NEED NOT BE SO. INDULGING YOUR mood with the use of color, treating familiar objects in imaginative ways, or just celebrating the simple beauty of food, all to create a memorable table setting, can be as gratifying as the process of planning and preparing a wonderful meal.

As Elizabeth and I have pulled together the ideas and images for *The Artful Table*, I have come to understand that our project is not only about setting the table but about seeing it. Our goal is to show you how to look at what you place on your table—even at the surface of the table itself, as well as the silverware, plates, glassware, linens, and centerpieces—in a fresh way.

Consider a simple wine goblet. Examine its shape. Observe its color. If it is crystal, consider how it looks empty . . . now filled with a pale yellow chardonnay . . . or a crimson beaujolais . . . how it might reflect sunlight or candlelight. That single glass has a relationship with every other object on the table. Now consider how it contrasts with fine porcelain, rugged stoneware, or metallic pewter.

Think of color, texture, pattern, and materials in terms of how each relates to the others. Consider the similarities and differences. For one table, we combined objects made from the same material, terra-cotta clay, produced in different shapes, styles, and origins. The earthy reds and the varying textures of the clays became part of the focus of the design. When placed on a piece of canvas painted a mossy-green color, and scattered among oddly colored natural objects such as plump green figs and large eggplant-colored leaves, the colors and subtle textures of the terra-cotta were enhanced. On another table, the intricate texture and implied grace of café-au-lait-colored lace is more notable against a slick metal table surface that reflects the delicacy of its

THE TABLE

weave and the softness of its color. Using a collection of monochromatic ceramics of dissimilar shapes, finished in a variety of glazes, emphasizes the tactile qualities of their matte and glossy surfaces. Spreading brightly colored silk shawls over a rough gray stone surface, or pairing coarse, craft-shop burlap with fine silk napkins and elegant sterling silver cutlery, emphasizes the contrast between the elements and materials while creating a visual harmony.

The same principles of contrast and unity apply to color as well. Keeping in mind a vision of the design as a whole, you might select a strong color—perhaps a deep jade or a brilliant crimson—as the basis for an entire table setting. Employ an intriguing combination of colors, or limit yourself to a specific palette to convey emotion or emphasize a feeling. The subtle color gradations in a bouquet of confetti roses, for example, are especially striking when the rest of the table is executed in a more soothing monochromatic palette of pale celadon greens. Combining familiar colors in an unexpected way can also be an interesting design challenge. Using strong

graphic shades of primary yellow, red, and blue in a sensual and sophisticated setting is a new presentation of a familiar concept. Consider different sources of inspiration—the season, the weather, your mood. A trip to the flower market or farm stand can provide new ideas. Or you might even limit yourself to one color and work with its emotional impact. On a cold winter evening, you might plan an entire meal and its setting in varying shades of warm, ochre-colored yellows. The result will be welcoming to both the eye and the spirit.

As a designer, I approach each project with the same aesthetic principles and problem-solving perspective. It is my tools that vary. I begin with a central theme, which for me often evolves organically. One crisp autumn morning, I noted how exquisite the vivid reds and golds of the leaves looked in the filtered sunlight of the early day. I wanted to interpret this observation as a way to share my pleasure with friends and planned a dinner party. Instead of the traditional trappings of fall— pumpkins and fallen leaves—I started with a neutral table and made a strong color statement with the food.

I covered a wooden table with a piece of woven raffia wallcovering (a remnant from another project), then placed a long, stripped branch down the center. Alongside, I set soft-white gourds. I chose heavy, hand-crafted plates in a putty-colored stoneware and used elegantly carved wooden cutlery.

In contrast, the foods I served were rich and vivid: yams in a deep burnt-orange, crimson roasted beets, a duck breast basted in a deep-red port wine sauce.

Just as you can be overwhelmed by the food when you sit down to a multiple-course meal and thereby lose appreciation for the artistry in each dish, so too can you lose sight of the essence of a design when there is too much on the table. I like a design that is strong and clear. In my own work, as a surface and textile designer, I often restrict myself to using only a few key elements to convey my idea. Restrictions may seem confining at first, but they usually help to keep me more focused.

It's good to experiment with new ideas by using objects, materials, or ingredients that are readily accessible and not too precious. You'll feel freer to experiment and less constrained by failure or waste. You might explore new table-covering possibilities by bunching or folding an inexpensive piece of cloth you find at a fabric store, instead of relying on ready-made tablecloths. You may be less likely to pull apart and scatter the petals from a bouquet of expensive flowers than from one of wildflowers from your own backyard. New ideas are born from experimentation.

Challenge yourself to find alternative uses for things. Vases may hold bread sticks or crackers, for instance. Condiments, nuts, and spices such as salt and cracked pepper are lovely in a special collection of small ceramic, paper, or wooden containers. A clear-glass lab beaker, filled with golden olive oil waiting to be drizzled on fresh bread, is an interesting alternative to the traditional bottle and spout. However, be sure that any unconventional use is both functional and sanitary. Before heaping a pile of mussel shells on the table, for example, I scrubbed and soaked them in hot water to remove sand, mud, and the smell of the seaside. Baskets should be clean, and possibly lined, if they are intended to hold food. Stones must be scrubbed, and branches and vines should be checked for debris and bugs. Fruits, vegetables, and any other edible items must be cleaned.

It is our hope that in reading, and, more important, looking at *The Artful Table*, you will not only find new, useful ideas, but you will begin to explore and discover some of your own. As you work to define and refine your own highly personal vision of what is beautiful, hopefully you will find pleasure in doing so and will experience enhancement of your everyday life.

SEATING OPTIONS

Almost without thinking, we rigidly adhere to convention about who should sit where. Families array themselves around the table. Married couples are separated at dinner parties. Men and women alternate. But these traditional ideas can be challenged. Keeping practical considerations in mind—number of guests, size and shape of the table—we can find many alternatives. For example, try seating diners at one end of the table, where they can focus on a wonderful object, a vase of flowers, or a display of beautiful food. If your dining room offers an enjoyable view, consider seating everyone along one side of the table so as to face it. If your table is long, you might arrange small conversational groupings. Do not sacrifice comfort, but try new seating arrangements to add to the overall success of your design.

SURFACES

For this book, we worked with three different table surfaces: wooden, brushed metal, and unfinished stone. Each table surface has its own characteristics, which must either be accounted for or eliminated altogether by using a tablecloth or other type of covering. The reflective character of metal or the soft patina of stone can enhance a design. Antique English Staffordshire ceramics combined with contemporary porcelain set atop a slick metal surface creates a montage, a contradiction that celebrates the diverse design of these objects. Soft, tactile felt has a very different character when paired with strong gray stone. A wooden surface peeking out from the edges of a river of bright-red linen adds an earthy quality to a design constructed around strong primary colors. Natural wood adds warmth and organic texture that a slick collection of contemporary ceramics and glassware might otherwise lack.

NONTRADITIONAL TABLE COVERINGS

Tablecloths are only one of many options for covering tables. Try laying sheets of metal, bark, burlap, silk, or lace over tables. Paint canvas or paper to create a specific design or obtain a particular color. You could even wrap tables in paper. Nontraditional materials can be interesting and economical, which is not always a goal in itself, but they can be helpful in facilitating the evolution of new ideas. Inexpensive scarves, rolls of paper, gauze dyed to a specific shade, and large pieces of handmade paper randomly laid over a table are all intriguing options. Instead of a traditional tablecloth, you might drape fabric, leaving the edges unfinished, over the top of the table or along one side. Layer pieces of fabric to create a focal point at one end of a table, or run a long narrow strip down the center. The color and texture of the cloth can be used to create movement, or to call attention to a particular area of the table.

You might also try devising some new table surfaces that can completely change the mood of a tabletop: slate patio tiles laid edge to edge; colorful ceramic bathroom tiles combined with highly textured cloth; or sheer yellow cotton batiste laid over the top of watercolor paper painted in the same shade.

NAPKINS

There are many creative alternatives to traditional napkins—scarves, squares of fabric cut from the table-covering yardage, woven linen hand towels, colorful handkerchiefs. The thick texture of a loosely woven fabric, the sharp surprise of a brightly colored piece of starched linen, or the simple drape of a beautiful swatch of silk are all possibilities. Napkins cut from a fabric remnant can be more economical than ready-made alternatives, allowing more room for experimentation

or a new idea. You might leave the fabric edges unfinished, or experiment with bindings or trims in different colors. Most often, I like to incorporate napkins subtly into the table setting so that they "disappear" rather than stand out. Selecting strong colors or intricate folds can make the napkins a stronger element of your table setting. Unlike a single centerpiece, they become a repetitive item in your design and should be part of your total plan.

NONTRADITIONAL DISPLAY ITEMS

I don't purchase traditional flower arrangements for my tables—the world is filled with too many other, more intriguing possibilities. You might try scattering flower petals or stones across a table, or artfully arranging long grasses atop a tablecloth. Dried magnolia leaves, first artfully arranged, then covered with a shimmering piece of sheer metallic fabric, create a "live" pattern across the table. Glassware or vases, empty or filled with unexpected objects or foods, can be beautiful. Display individual fruits or vegetables, or small groupings, along the table surface like small sculptures, or display charcoal-gray stones on a black-and-cream-colored cloth, or vivid green plums mimicking the acid-green glaze of the porcelain plate upon which they are about to be served. Don't worry about whether the displays or your color palette are related to the food.

FOOD AS A DISPLAY ITEM

Celebrate the simple beauty of food by incorporating it into your table designs. Bound branches of pomegranates or vines of ripening blackberries can be as beautiful as any bouquet of roses. A sculpted winter squash striped with soft green and yellow, a small pile of fresh fava bean pods, or a head of magenta-colored radicchio, peeled so that it resembles a flower—these are all objects of simple, natural beauty. I have stacked eggs in a crystal vase and placed them at the center of a table, not because they had any specific theme or relevance to the meal, but just to enjoy their luminous purity and shape.

FLOWERS AND OTHER NATURAL DISPLAYS

A large bunch of French tulips in soft sunset shades can establish a mood, and the color itself is worthy of a painting. Appreciate flowers purely for their color, shape, and texture, rather than for any innate association they might represent. Experiment with the patterns and shapes created by assorted bunches, such as dahlias, Gerber daisies, lilacs, and hydrangeas. Use fruits, twigs, herbs, and other unexpected elements from the earth, and apply them to a table setting in a nonthematic way. Several perfect, pale oyster mushrooms placed in a bowl as a centerpiece can be as elegant as a grouping of orchids, since their odd shapes, subtle color variations, and soft edges evoke such delicacy. Emphasizing the sculptural quality of a single long, spare branch by using it to define the space on a table is an elegant tribute to nature. Exotic fruits and flowers can be wonderful contributions to your design, but consider instead the beauty of twisting vines of wild grapes, a bouquet of small branches about to burst into bloom, or leaves from a favorite tree in your yard. The yard is full of possibilities. So are the woods, the seashore, and other natural settings. When I combined the pile of mussel shells foraged from a recent trip to the seashore with antique silver and a shimmering river of purple taffeta, it was the contrast of the materials as well as the similarities in color and texture that created such an effective combination.

CENTERPIECES AND OTHER MEANS OF DISPLAY

I think of the "center" of the table as the common area that brings diners together. Consider which area of the table to use (don't rule out corners) and how you might employ this space to unite your design or establish a focal point. An oversized wedge of golden Parmesan cheese, placed directly on a paper table covering, from which guests can break off small wedges, or an "art piece" bowl typically reserved for display, but instead used to serve olives or nuts, are both good examples. A large wooden tray in the middle of the table, piled high with beautiful fresh breads, can be a "centerpiece" in the traditional sense. Gather assorted serving pieces at one corner of the table, artfully place vases and bowls down the length of the table, or stack a grouping of small plates together in the middle. Depending on where you seat your guests, you may want the end of the table to be your focal point. A tall terra-cotta bowl perched on the end of the table, piled high with colorful blood oranges, can attract the eye as effectively as a traditional floral arrangement in the center.

GLASSWARE

As objects, expensive stemware may be beautiful, but it is not always the most interesting solution. Consider the fluid, waterlike quality of a clear glass, or the textural artistic strokes on a hand-glazed cup. The characteristics of all materials offer another opportunity to contribute to your total design. Serve a soft, pink-colored rosé wine in a low, delicate cocktail glass to add to both the color and mood. Tall chartreuse crystal goblets are especially notable when placed in a stark white setting, where exploring texture is the focus. Small glazed terra-cotta mugs, or Japanese porcelain teacups, can serve wine, water, or other beverages for which they were not originally intended. Thick, heavy, colored glasses, depending on their shade or scale, can imply one idea, whereas delicate crystal goblets with an etched texture or pattern can convey another. Mixing contemporary and antique can also be interesting, but age and origin are irrelevant unless the objects themselves have the visual effect you are striving for.

DINNERWARE

Like all other elements in your design, dinnerware must be carefully considered, but first and foremost as the vehicle for food. In my mind, that is where the primary visual emphasis should always be. I often use oversized plates—portions seem grander and more special when displayed on a large canvas, so to speak. Solid-colored or glass plates, depending on the color or scale, fit into most any table setting. The transparency of glass is most helpful when I want the plates to "fall away" so as to emphasize the food itself and the surface beneath it.

Innovative table coverings such as the petals of a flower or a large green leaf, when placed under a glass plate, can be the visual focus of a place setting and an unusual backdrop for food. Try mixing sizes, patterns, and styles—but when doing so, work toward some kind of continuity, since the plates are another repetitive element in the design. You might combine different shapes in a similar color or material, or place assorted patterned plates atop similar ones in a larger scale.

CUTLERY

I liken cutlery to jewelry: It should be used as an object of visual interest, or fall away and become unnoticeable. Because even inexpensive cutlery is often quite an investment, eating utensils cannot be changed as easily as table coverings, plates, or napkins. Unless you have several sets to choose from, a simple pattern of cutlery that flatters most table settings, or visually falls away, is usually best. Carved wood, tarnished antique silver, or aged yellow Bakelite, however, are all interesting materials that can be a beautiful addition to a table-setting idea.

LIGHTING

Lighting is critically important in conveying a mood. Think about the time of day, the season, and the nature of your setting in planning how (or even how) you will light your table. Outdoor dining under the moon and stars, twilight cocktails in the autumn, even late afternoon gatherings in the winter, all present their own ambience. Ambient light can create a sense of drama much more effectively than electric lights or even candles. However, natural light is usually not enough. You may want to add candles, small lamps, natural light, torchlights, or overhead lighting. Be aware not only of the overall effect but of how the light will fall upon the individual diners. To minimize glare, use low-wattage bulbs. Candles are always most convenient, because you can place them along the length of the table, or concentrate them in a specific area where you would like more light.